O Jesus

Prayers
from the Diaries of
Catherine de Hueck Doherty

with an introduction by
Lorene Hanley Duquin

MADONNA HOUSE | PUBLICATIONS
Combermere, Ontario | Canada   K0J 1L0

I had the privilege of reading Catherine's diaries when I was working on research for the biography I wrote, *They Called Her the Baroness*. When I started the research, I was a marginal Catholic with shallow beliefs and casual connections to the Church. I had been writing dramatic narratives about people's lives for secular women's magazines, and I knew that I could not enter into Catherine's life on an emotional level without getting caught up in her pain. What I did not realize was that I would also enter Catherine's life on a spiritual level and would discover God.

Reading someone else's diaries is intensely personal. In Catherine's, raw honesty rips through the pages, and when I paralleled the content of her spiritual journals with her day–to–day activities, I saw how the physical, emotional and intellectual sides of this woman interwove themselves with her faith life.

For the first time in my life, God became real. I could feel his presence on those pages. I could see the way the Holy Spirit nudged Catherine with ideas and insights, and yet never forced her to do anything. I saw how Catherine's prayers were answered. I watched as deep spiritual insights unraveled before my eyes. I saw her grow in understanding, in knowledge, in truth, in wisdom.

I couldn't read her examinations of conscience without examining my own. I trembled at her temptations and wept over her weaknesses. I became acutely aware of my own shortcomings as I saw her struggle to break bad habits, to control her temper, to be more truthful, to have more patience.

I found myself praying with Catherine, joining my intentions with hers, and begging for light, for truth, for understanding in my own life. I learned to meditate by reading her meditations.

I could see that during her times of spiritual dryness, when Catherine had no conscious perception of God's presence, the Holy Spirit was alive and working in her life. I learned what it means to walk in blind faith as I watched Catherine grope her way through spiritual darkness with only enough light to move one step at a time.

I watched when many times Catherine seemed to overflow with an awareness of God's love, and responded to that divine love by reaching out to help other people. She saw the lonely, suffering Christ in others, and she felt a burning desire to ease their pain and comfort them.

Catherine kept diaries for over sixty years. What you will see in this volume are excerpts from her prayers over a seven year period in the mid-1930's. All references to specific people, places or events have been edited out. What remains is a concentrated dose of Catherine's spirituality and how it developed.

The first prayer in this volume is from July 1931. Others follow starting in June 1933, when Catherine was investigating the spread of Communism in Toronto for Archbishop Neil McNeil. The prayers continue through the opening of Friendship House in Toronto, the tensions that led to its closing, and into Catherine's time of doubts and despair as she struggled to rebuild her life afterward. The book leaves her in June 1938, shortly after her arrival in Harlem, New York, and the beginning of her Interracial Apostolate.

In this book, you will find no biographical notes or explanations. If you are interested in details of Catherine's life during this time, you can find them in any of the biographies that have been written about her. The purpose of this book is not to examine Catherine's life. Instead, it gives you an opportunity to step into her soul in a way that is personal and private.

As you read there may be times when the prayers will flow over you like a gentle breeze. At other times, they will batter you like a bitter wind. Some of the prayers will cause you to think about your own life. Some will challenge you to look at your strengths and weaknesses. Some will bring new insights. Others will reinforce old truths. All of them will call you to a deeper relationship with Jesus Christ.

Take your time when reading these prayers. Pause. Reflect. Feel free to interweave your own doubts, fears, temptations, sufferings, hopes, and joys into Catherine's, and into the words and images in which she expressed them.

Her prayers from this period are essentially a collection of meditations. She would read from Scripture or from spiritual classics, take one line or idea from what she read, and then write her own meditation. You may recognize quotes and ideas on these pages from St. Ignatius Loyola, St. Francis de Sales, and from lesser known sources such as *The Soul of the Apostolate* by Dom Jean-Baptiste Chautard, OCSO; *God With Us* by Fr. Raoul Plus, SJ; *The Virtue of Trust* by Fr. Paul de Jaegher, SJ; *In the Likeness of Christ* and *Progress Through Mental Prayer* by Fr. Edward Leen, CSSp, and *Abandonment* by Fr. Jean-Pierre de Caussade, SJ.

You will note that one of Catherine's most fervent prayers was that she would always follow God's will. She was acutely aware that she could not accomplish anything on her own, and this theme reverberates throughout.

Another interesting spiritual phenomenon was the way Catherine saw her own sinfulness in relation to the blinding brilliance of God's perfect goodness. It may startle you that Catherine, who gave so much in the service of other people, saw herself as having done very little.

She held nothing back in examining her conscience. She sometimes referred to sins of her past, absolved long before but for which she still had a deep desire to make reparation. She struggled with habitual faults and weaknesses, such as her tendencies toward boasting, sarcasm, exaggeration, impatience, irritability, and impulsiveness. She tried to offset these by cultivating the virtues of kindness, compassion, gentleness, and love.

We know from classical theology that there are three sources of temptation: the world, the flesh, and the devil. If you look closely, you will see mention of all these sources of temptation in Catherine's prayers. She had given up the glamor and luxury of the world for a life of voluntary poverty, but there were times when she grew weary of the constant presence of people in her life. She knew that she had the talents to return to the world where she could have made money and lived a life of self-gratification. It was only by clinging to her conviction that God had called her to work with the poor that she overcame the temptation to return to a worldly, self-centered existence.

Some of Catherine's temptations were sexual. She was a passionate, physical person, and even though her marriage had sometimes been abusive, she had known the joys and pleasures of intimate sexual contact. During these years, Catherine struggled with her withdrawal from sexual pleasure and her body craved human touch. She fought this craving by begging for strength and offering her temptations as a sacrifice.

You will also find that some of Catherine's temptations stemmed from lies implanted in her consciousness by forces of evil. These insidious lies attempted to destroy her relationship with Jesus Christ—by confusing her with uncertainty, disorienting her with distorted perceptions of reality, overwhelming her with negativity, and leading her toward thoughts of hopelessness or despair. For example, she often received acclaim for her work, and was tempted to think that perhaps it was self-glory and hunger for praise that fueled her desire to live in poverty and serve the poor, and not love of God at all. She prayed often for "purity of intention," and begged to be stripped of pride and vanity.

The greatest tool Catherine used in overcoming temptation was the Sacrament of Reconciliation. In the confessional, priests always led her to the infinite mercy of God. Catherine seemed to know in the marrow of her bones that in spite of her weaknesses and her sinfulness, God loved her passionately. She seemed perplexed at times that someone as unworthy as herself would be called to serve the Lord. She prayed often for an increased love of God. She also prayed to become a saint—not the public kind of saint, you will notice—but a small, hidden one. She knew that in order to become a saint, she had to undergo a stripping away of everything in her that was not of God. "Make me a saint," she prayed repeatedly, "and do not spare me in the making."

During this time, Catherine also came to a growing awareness of the weaknesses of priests. At times she was overwhelmed with pain at the way so many of them chose to live in luxury when people in their own parishes were homeless and hungry. She saw the human side of the church, and she begged for the grace not to judge anyone.

Catherine understood that following Christ always leads to crucifixion. On a human level, she reeled in horror at pain, but on a spiritual level, she begged for the strength to follow in the footsteps of Jesus. Deep in her soul she knew that through suffering she would be more closely united to him. You will find her praying frequently for the will to bear persecution, criticism, and betrayal.

Throughout all of this, Jesus Christ was Catherine's only source of hope and consolation. There were times when Jesus was her only friend, the only one she could talk to, the only one she could count on to understand.

Catherine was not a perfect person. She suffered. She struggled. She made mistakes. Sometimes she triumphed over her temptations; sometimes she succumbed to them. But she never stopped trying to be better, and Christ became ever more deeply the center of her life.

I believe that in this collection of Catherine's prayers there is a strong message of faith, hope and love. It is my greatest hope that as you step into the soul of Catherine de Hueck Doherty, your faith, your hope, and your love will move to a deeper level, and that God in his infinite love and mercy will touch you in the same ways that he touched Catherine.

Lorene Hanley Duquin
May 1996

O Jesus

I Offer You My Soul

Dear Jesus, You said several words on the cross. As I ponder them, one stands out: "I am thirsty."[1] You thirst for souls.

Your thirst was not for water, cool and limpid as it might have been. It was for the soul, for the limpidity of human love, for the coolness of a loving touch. You thirst for love, incomprehensible as this may seem—for the love of men and women.

O Lord, do not permit me to tarry even a moment once I hear Your cry. Allow me, the greatest sinner of all, to answer it. Let me spend the rest of my life trying to quench Your thirst for souls. Let me offer You my soul and lead to You the souls of others. (July 30, 1931)

I Come to You

O Jesus, my mind is blank, but I had to come to You. The emptiness inside of me made me come. There was nothing left. Where could I replenish the lack of all? Only at Your feet. So I came. It was not easy. It was hard. But what is easy in the way of serving God? (June 29, 1933)

Look at prisoners, people deprived of their liberty, how unhappy they are! But to You, dear Lord, who are Love, this great gift of my liberty is nothing compared to what You have done and are doing. Jesus, O my Jesus! What is liberty? Why do I need it when I am a slave of Love? I love You. Teach me to love You more and more. Gladly do I relinquish my liberty to You, ashamed only of my niggardliness: I give so little when I have received so much. (July 5, 1933)

The Last Judgment
Think, my soul, of the Last Judgment! No appeal, no possibility to atone, naked before the eyes of God—in an awful nakedness—for every thought, every word, every deed will stand revealed! How we should watch over them now!

The most terrible ordeal of all will be the revelation of God's Love—its immensity, its beauty, its loveliness—all lost! And for what? For a moment of bitter earthly satisfaction. How tragic and how final. Like a bird afraid will our souls flutter and dream of what would have been but never now will be! O, while there is still time, work, my soul, for the ineffable joy of being admitted to God's elect.

When am I going to die? Who knows? Perhaps I have only yet a little time. How full of sin I am, how utterly unworthy, O my Lord. (July 6, 1933)

Nothing Is More Beautiful than Christ
"He is the desire of the everlasting hills." (see *Gn 49:26*)

Nothing in this world is more beautiful than Christ. The lessons of His earthly life have never been surpassed in high idealism. But how hard it is for me to follow in His footsteps! Daily, hourly, my human frailty clashes with my desire to follow Him. O Lord! You see how weak I am, how easily tired of all the glory of eternity when it means a daily grind against sins, passions and desires of my body.

I love You, O Christ, with a love as great as I am capable of. But my deeds belie my words. What am I to do? I know only one remedy. It is to come to You in Holy Communion, ashamed, poor, utterly unworthy—to come because You have called me, because without You I am nothing, because my love of You will never grow without Your help, my passions never be overcome.

O Lord behold me, a sinner who yet has loved You all her life. I have, my Lord! Never have I forgotten You entirely. But, O Jesus, this will be my condemnation: the graces You have sent me, have I corresponded with them? Far from it! I have neglected them. Forgive me, O Lord and God. Forgive me and receive me back into Your arms where alone I find happiness, dear Christ.

Teach me to live by the day. Teach me to be kind in word, thought, deed. Teach me to be poor, to serve You well by serving well Your poor. Help me, O Lord, to overcome myself just for today. O Jesus, have mercy on me a sinner!

(July 7, 1933)

O Lord, Enter My Soul

"Behold I stand at the gate and knock." (*Rv 3:20*)

My Lord, do not look at my closed door. Touch it and it will open! Help of the sick, come in. How strange it seems that You, Jesus, Almighty God, could do such a thing—"stand and knock" at the door of my soul!

I am so terribly unworthy. The thing still more astounding is that few choose You, or even hear that knock and answer that invitation. And the few who do, how clean are their hearts? Look at me, O Lord, look at me! Desolate is my heart. O Jesus, help me to clean it; as long as I live, help me not to despair. Amen.

(July 11, 1933)

Seek Me, for I Am Lost

O Lord, seek me, for I am lost. Lost in the maze of life, passions, temptations! I seem to do nothing but fail. Have pity on me, my Lord. Help me. Forgive me. Help me. Help me.

(July 12, 1933)

To Be Like Children

"Become like little children." (*Mt 18:3*)

How true and profound a saying! Children have innocence, love, simplicity, trustfulness, eagerness, joyfulness, truthfulness. Like little children! How hard it is to be like one when one is grown up.

Mercy on me, O Lord, is all I ask.   (July 13, 1933)

Save Me, Lord

Save me, O Lord, from myself, from the concupiscence of the world, from the mud of it. Jesus! Without You, I am lost. Make me understand! O my Lord and my God! You are the Alpha and Omega of my life; let me seek only You! For it is only when my soul is at peace with You that I feel happy. Save me, my Lord, for I am Yours.   (July 21,1933)

Trust

"Trials are melting pots in which our trust is discovered and refined." (*1 Pet 1:7*)

My Lord, teach me to trust You absolutely, infinitely, without a moment's hesitation, the way I used to when I was younger. It is so easy for children to trust. Make me like a child, O my Lord.

O Jesus, help me, for without Your help I am nothing.

(August 1, 1933)

I Will Trust in Your Mercy

O Jesus, I wish that perfect trust existed in me, that I could say fully that in the future I will be good. But O Lord, You know it is impossible. What am I to do then? Why is it impossible? Because I do not trust in Your mercy. Forgive me, my Lord, and teach me to love more and to trust more.

(September 8, 1933)

My Soul Is Dark

O God, Your light is dimmed. Somehow the road is lonely again. I imagine I deserve all this and much more, for of late I have begun to forget prayers and Masses and all the things I should be doing.

My Lord, let me repeat again and again: "All for the greater glory of God."

Never let me forget that all I can ever be is a pliable instrument in Your hand. Teach me to pray first and do afterward. This is the main point in life—prayers and penance first, and then only, works. (November 11, 1933)

Forty Hours Devotion

O God, I went to Mass today. How full of beauty is the Church—eternal, glorious beauty! What a privilege is the Roman Catholic Church. It is a gem beyond any understanding, a lover beyond any comparison. As I knelt before the Blessed Sacrament it was as if music of inexplicable charm filled my ears. My heart was full to overflowing with the love of Him who is forever so gentle with me, so forbearing! So patient! O Jesus, do not allow me to leave You. (November 13, 1933)

The Last Day of the Year

Another year gone into the chasm of eternity! What have I done with it, my Lord and my God? Today at Mass, You vouchsafed to me a glimpse of my nothingness, my utter inadequacy, my hopelessness in Your service.

How can You, my Lord, have patience with such as I? I know Your patience and mercy are infinite. But look at my vanity, self–love, indulgences of all kinds! Look at the graces You showered on me, and look at the lack of cooperation on my part.

Look at my unworthiness; look at Your kindness, Jesus, Son of Man, my Lord and my God. Forgive me and accept my thanks for allowing me another chance. I know my weakness. I know that without You I am nothing. Help me! Alone I cannot make one step. Let me see myself as I am.

Make me realize these graces that You have allowed. Give me tolerance, understanding, humility, patience! Above all, inflame my heart with an unquenchable love for You. Make me an alert servant, not a sloppy, tired, lazy one as I have been until now. Do not allow me, sweet Lord, to take unto myself any pride about my achievement; make me humbly realize that I am only an instrument. You know it is all for Your glory.

Make me more charitable, more gentle, more understanding with people. Give me humility—then I shall be able to serve You as I must. Cure my laziness. Give me strength and determination for sacrifices and mortifications. Make me patient, controlling all irritability, anger, impatience.

Help me, O Master. Look not at the unworthiness of Your servant but only on her desire to serve You. Enkindle that desire until, as a flame, it consumes me entirely! Bless all the things I do in Your name. Give me understanding of what I should do and what I should run away from. Give me Your love! In temporal things, give me my daily bread, and the rest as You will. Your will be done, not mine.   (December 31, 1933)

A New Year

Dear Jesus, I have done so little for You in the past year. I do not know what You have in store for me for this year, yet I accept it with its joys, sacrifices, sorrow, pain and even death—joyfully—for it is Your choice.

You will help me to do my part and cooperate with Your grace, refrain from my habitual sins, overcome my faults and defects. O Jesus, You know that without You I am nothing. Be with me! Allow me to spend this coming year in Your love and service, without counting the cost.

Bless me and my family, those with whom I come into contact—especially those who dislike me. They have good reasons. Bring to Your feet those who seek You, groping for Your Light.

Bless and help the dying, the poor, the sick I deal with. Give the gift of holiness to all the priests I know and also the religious. Bless all those who love me and help me. Give strength, health and wisdom to the Pope and Bishops. Bless this house and all who are in it. Let me always remember that all that I am, all that I have are Yours. (January 1, 1934)

Give Me Peace

"Come, Lord. Visit on us peace that we might rejoice before You." (*Ps 106:4,5*)

Sweet Lord, give me the peace of Your Holy Spirit, the peace where nothing troubles me in my tiring day. Grant that when I am overburdened, the thought of Your peace may come—beautiful and calming. The little irritations of this world are like needle pricks. Give me the strength not to notice them. Give me the peace of my faith that no worldly assault may shake.

Help me. Bless me. Let me radiate Your peace, Jesus of Nazareth, that in this impatient world Your peace might be the peace of a turbulent sea quieted by Your Word.

(January 2, 1934)

Let Me Pass Your Peace to Others

Sweet Lord, help me always to have and to pass on to others the peace which You alone can give. O Jesus, without You I can do nothing. With You, I can do everything! Be with me always, sweet, peaceful Lord. Help me always to consider my neighbor, to mortify myself without showing it, to hold back my words that might hurt, to never speak ill of my neighbor. With Your peace, give me the necessary humility to hold my peace and give me the tears to weep over my sins for they hurt You, my sweet Lord. (January 3, 1934)

Love of Neighbor

Love of neighbor! Is that not Your beloved commandment? Is it not the fullness of the Law, the characteristic of Your true

stress should be placed on spiritual food for those out of work. They are in the darkness of despair. Surely we can, we must, help them to find You. Build without You and I build on sand.

In my work, I do my best to lead the person to You, for I know it is You who send me in the first place. It is You who will do the rest. (April 19, 1934)

Sinfulness
It seems to me that sin is like a magic cloak. No sooner do we divest ourselves of it, than that moment does it seem to come back again. Evade it, and it will follow you into the desert. Run into the crowded street; it is with you again. All around you it is, so hard to get rid of, so hard to steal away from.

Only one refuge is left—the Lord! Help me, Jesus. Help me. Help! (April 20, 1934)

To Preach the Gospel
My Lord, to preach the Gospel to heathens is a marvelous achievement, but here at home there is another work to be done. Your own disciples have forgotten You. The darkness of these lean days has shadowed Your face for many. You are forgotten when You should be most remembered. Doctrines as dark or darker than those of the pagans are being spread about.

It is high time that people remember the Light of Christ. Your Light. Let it shine into the distressed world. Let it bring deep understanding and lighten the burden. Let it shine especially in the dark corners of people's hearts, driving selfishness and greed out of them.

Help me, dear Lord, to be one of those who will go and tell the world. (April 21, 1934)

To Preach with My Life
"People study your life, not your words. See then that your life does not belie your teachings."

My Jesus, seldom have I come across a better meditation than this one. My whole life is just that. You know how I want to work for You. You know how I love You. But look at my work. It never amounts to much because my life does not amount to much. Teach me to be really humble, really charitable, really patient in little deeds, not just in big ones. Just slowly, simply. Let me see what others can learn from my life, not only from my words. (April 27, 1934)

The Peace of Christ

My Jesus, peace is what I need most. Your peace, not the world's, so that I might move in the midst of the turmoil of life at peace with myself and all others. Jesus, Son of Man, grant me peace. There is so much strife around me that without Your peace I will not be able to go on. Help me, Jesus. Help me never to be afraid, never to stop because of fear of others and their judgment. Your judgment is the only one I value. Help me, O Jesus. (April 28?, 1934)

The World Has Ceased to Know You, Lord

Dear Jesus, the world has ceased to know You. Busy straightening out things without You, they wonder why they do not come to any good results. It is simply because You are not here. And we, who do not think we can help, are not fulfilling Your desire to let Your light shine before the world.

Jesus, how often I wander far from You even when working for You. Look at me shouting, doing, talking, teaching, feeling proud and good! Am I doing anything? Who can say? I am not doing the principal thing: praying and being quiet. How much better would I see things if I prayed to You more, my Lord. Help me to understand. Help me to see that often it is in doing nothing that one does most.

Jesus, my God! Teach me to be a lamp with You as the oil. Help me always to shine brightly for others to see. Help me.

(May 3, 1934)

Little Things

O Jesus, let me gather up all fragments lest they be lost. Let me never pass by the most insignificant thing without thinking of You. A look, a word, and behold—another person has been drawn to You!

Let me be attentive to each and everyone, everywhere. I thank You for yesterday's opportunities. Help me to see and not miss today's. O Jesus, be my light. (May 5, 1934)

To Be with You

My dear Jesus, how can I thank You for this grace of being allowed, no, invited, to come apart and spend a little while with You. How I have longed for silence and solitude! I am so tired of people, so tired of them all. Yet I love them still and they are still precious to me.

Jesus, I am sorely perplexed. Please, my dear Lord, give me the light to see and understand. You know what I need. I am all astray! Put me right. Give me light. And when I see, give me strength to do Your work against all and everyone.

(May 25, 1934)

Sin

My God, give me the grace of realizing that sin is the most terrible thing in the whole world. Make me realize why it is so terrible. It has crucified You, our God! It crucifies You still, anew and anew! O Victim of Love! It is because we have the crucifix that we have life! Help me, O Jesus, help me to realize the enormity of sin: Your death was necessary to liberate us from its eternal punishment.

How can I sin when it crucifies my Savior? O Jesus, with tears I cry: "Have mercy on me, a sinner!" (May 27, 1934)

I Look over My Life

Dear Jesus, I look over my life. All I see is sin, sin of every kind. Only You know how full of sin my life has been. I have no refuge anywhere from my sins, except in the sacrament of Your peace and mercy. Why is it that You have given me the grace of time, yet a little while in which to make penance for my sins and, above all, receive absolution for them? Jesus, Son of Man, have mercy on me a sinner.

I have loved You since babyhood. I have tried to run away from You, O Lord, many times. But You have delighted in bringing such an unworthy servant back. Jesus, give me the grace to stay with You now that I am back. Give me sorrow that I might weep over my sins. Give me a humble and contrite heart.

O Jesus, for all my sins I cry profoundly. So, with Your grace, I propose not to commit them any more. Help me, O Jesus, help me.   (May 28, 1934)

Preparation for Confession

"The fruit of confession is the forgiveness of God and His utter forgetfulness of Your sin."

O Jesus, what a consoling thought! It is so hard to think that this is possible, so hard to imagine such goodness. But all God's attributes are hard to imagine. Jesus, have mercy on me a sinner.
                              (May 28, 1934)

O Holy Spirit

O Holy Spirit, guide me into the path of salvation. I love You; I want to love You evermore. Help me! I am working for You in a haphazard way, with dark shadows of sin crossing the sunny places of my little efforts. Eliminate these shadows, O Spirit of Light.

Your holy will has placed me in the limelight of the world. Help me never to glory in any of its adulation. It is like sand scattered by the winds of the desert. Through Your will I have a certain influence over people; I can help them, be it ever so little.

Above all, be my light. Take my will, my understanding, my memory, all of me. Fashion and mold me to serve You alone.

Foster and nurture my devotion to You, O Third Person of the Trinity. Touch me with the fiery tongue of longing for absolute truth, absolute love. (May 28, 1934)

God Is Everywhere

God is everywhere. I meet Him in the slums, in my reading, in my meditations. Jesus is in me. I am in His grace. O Lord and Savior, give all! (May 31?, 1934)

Strengthen My Trust, Lord

"In You, O Lord, I have hoped. Let me not be confounded." (*Ps 31:1*)

Dear Jesus, in the midst of our saving, insuring, thrifty world of today, it seems foolish to trust even in God! Yet, somehow, deep, deep in my soul, I know there is no one to trust but You. Teach me to see Your hand in all the things that come to me. Teach me to see it in happiness and in so-called "reverses." For in them, often, are hidden real treasures.

Beloved Jesus, You know my inclination. You know how I long to trust You all the way. Do not allow the world with its stingy ways to shear this trust of mine. The world foolishly trusts in silver and gold—here today and gone tomorrow. I, Jesus, want to trust You like a child, to put my hand in Yours and walk the road of life with its ups and downs under the shadow of Your will. In all things that I cannot control, help me to do Your will. (June 4, 1934)

Teach Me to Believe

"All things are possible to faith." (*Mk 9:23*)

Yes, O Lord. So they are. But faith is Your gift, Your supreme gift to mankind. How to develop it, to cultivate it, to enlarge that faith is the thing. Teach me, my Jesus, how to do it. Teach me to believe. Teach me trust without end.

(June 9, 1934)

My Heart Magnifies the Lord

"My heart magnifies the Lord, for He has done great things." (*Lk 1:46,49*)

O Jesus, how shall I thank You for Your graces, for Your kindness, for the wonder of it all—that I should be chosen to have even a little part in Your work! Help me to understand a little of Your truth. Help me to conform my will to Yours. Help me to be humble. Help me to throw self-glorification absolutely away, remembering always: God delights to choose the most vile instruments for His glorification. O Jesus, help me, forgive me and bless me.

(June 13, 1934)

Learn from Me

Jesus, help me to be meek and humble, especially when a little success has come in my work! Jesus help me; do not allow shallow feelings of self-glorification to creep in. Help me always to remember that in all things, I am nothing. Help me to see straight and plan straight. Bless my day.

(June 14, 1934)

Spend Yourself in Love

"Work for Jesus; to Him be devoted; spend yourself in love."[2]

Dear Lord, this is my desire: to devote all my life to You. I have to hurry and crowd two days into every day, as I know not when will be the last. I want to spend myself in Your service, for Your glory. Help me, O Jesus, to do so. Because even though I work for You in others and for others, there is my own soul in which meekness, humility, conformity to Your will, trust and many other virtues must be developed.

O Jesus, help me. Implant in me such a desire to please You that nothing will matter but You. O Lord of heaven and earth, teach me to become a saint and do not spare me in the teaching.

(June 19, 1934)

May I Hide Myself in You

Dear Jesus, may I dissolve myself in Your will. May I hide myself in You, leaving to You all the things in my life. O Jesus, I love You. Teach me how to love You more, evermore, until, incapable of carrying the burden of longing, I might at last be freed.

O Jesus, help me to be a saint, for the other meaning of a saint is a lover of God. Jesus, make me that—a lover of God, a servant of love. Teach me never to hesitate in service to You, never to spare myself the mortification of interrupted peace, of eternal contact with people. Teach me how to overcome likes and dislikes—in You. Teach me to submit my life to You. Teach me to lose myself in You. (June 20, 1934)

I Am Yours

Once and for all, all my works, thoughts, suffering—in a word, my life—are for You, Jesus, in a humble, small reparation for my sins.

I ask for a conformity to Your will. In sorrow, in joy, in perseverance, in praise, in life and death, I want to bless Your will. I ask, again, my Jesus, for meekness, for humility and, above all, for charity. Make me really fond of people because I want to be consumed in loving You, my Lord. Give me Your most precious gift of all—a burning, insatiable love of You—so that, strengthened by that love, I may spend my life in Your service—not to gain heaven, not to escape hell, but because I love You!

O Jesus, see how weak we are! Without You we are nothing, just nothing. Help us. Save us. Be with us. In Your wounds, hide us! (June 24, 1934)

Thanksgiving: for the Eucharist

Dear Jesus, my heart sings the song of thanksgiving! And I think of how inadequate our hearts are in expressing our feelings to You. O Lord of my soul, I prostrate myself before You at the mere thought of the Blessed Sacrament. What infinite mystery is this! O Jesus, gratitude overflows my heart. The world without the Eucharist would be an empty world indeed.

Jesus, be blessed in the Sacrament of the Altar, now and forever! Help me to worship You. (June 29, 1934)

My Heart Is Heavy

Jesus, dear Jesus. I am so tired today, so terribly tired. All I want to do is sleep. There is no desire in me to get up, to go to church, to Communion. My heart is heavy within me. Yesterday evening's prayers were like a stone around my neck. Forgive me, Jesus. I will try again. The only thing that keeps me to my rule of life is my will. I wonder, Jesus, what Your will is. Somehow, my thoughts are muddled today. O Jesus, help me.

(June 30, 1934)

Jesus, Teach me

Dear Jesus, I love You. I believe in You. Teach me to show this love and belief in my daily life. Teach me to live in You. Teach me to teach others this love and belief! Without it, I am nothing. In You, I am all.

Let my faith and love bring forth fruits of love and faith. For only then will they be true. Jesus, make me realize my need of sanctification. Teach me how to pray, how to mortify myself, how to deal with others.

O Jesus, I love You. Make me show my love in tenderness for humanity. Help me to overcome myself, never counting the cost.

O Jesus, be in me, with me, around me. (July 1, 1934)

To Be Faithful in Little Things

Jesus, we all dream of big, heroic actions for Your sake. Teach us to be ready for them if they come. And show us the value of little, daily humble things done well. Teach me to understand the depth of the saying, "Be you faithful in little things"[3]—a word suppressed, a smile given, a weakness overcome. They, too, can win heaven for someone. Teach me to do them. Teach me to remember the thirty years of hidden life You lived before the three public years of Your miracles. Let me also see the beauty of hidden life that is to be found in lowly tasks of life.

Jesus, teach me the greatness of little things!   (July 1, 1934)

Forgive Me My Tiredness

Dear Jesus, today I've had a rest. I did not mean to miss Mass. I just overslept. Forgive me, dear Mary, Mother of God, for it is one of your feast days and I meant with all my heart to go. The spirit was willing, the flesh weak.[4]   (July 2, 1934)

The Good Shepherd

"Jesus, no one can frighten me, for I know so well what to believe concerning Your mercy and Your love!" (St. Theresa of Lisieux)[5]

You see my soul—weak, vacillating, needy, sick, tired, filled with longings, lacking all virtues. You are the physician of souls. Here is one that is very sick, so sick that You leave Your ninety-nine just sheep and go forth to find me.

Yet, instead of greeting You happily and running toward You, I make a few steps backward, for I am blind and cannot see the fathomless depths behind me.

So You stop. And, in Your sweet, kind way, You call me. Even my hardened heart cannot resist the call of Your voice. Irresolutely, I leave the cliff's edge; with lowered head and recalcitrant steps, I make my way toward You. You bend and take me in Your arms, whispering, "You are mine; you cannot wander away. I died for you. Come back to me."

Something breaks in my heart, some heavy burden is lifted from my soul, and I realize that I am Yours; adoring You, I nestle closer to Your heart and we start, together, our journey back.

After awhile, when I have been warmed at the fire of Your love, You put me down and say, trustingly and simply, "Follow me."

And now You choose, slowly, such a hard road. From nowhere, it seems, a heavy burden is placed upon my shoulder—a cross. You disappear sometimes at the turn of a road. The burden nearly breaks my back when I do not see You. I stumble and fall again. I have nothing to guide me but the imprints of Your feet. At times, as I lie in the dust of the road, I think I never shall have the strength to get up. But, at that very moment, You are near again, and the cross ceases to be heavy. The burden is there no more. You share it with me.

So goes life—darkness, almost despair, again light, again shadows—Your flitting presence to my senses, Your abiding presence to my faith.

I know I cannot turn back. I have heard the beating of Your heart. I have realized Your love for me. I will follow You, with Your help, unto the end.

The graces You send me are here because I am so weak. Others can rely on their good lives, their good works. I, only on You. For I have nothing to offer You except that love which You kindled in my heart one dark night when I was at the edge of a precipice.

O Jesus, let nothing separate us anymore. I walk in darkness, lit only by faith. Make mine a strong and unshakable faith.

(July 2, 1934)

All of Us Are Beggars

"All of us are beggars—beggars of the King of Kings."[6]

Jesus, this, at last, is a just word: beggar. That is what we are to You, beggars—ragged, filthy, tired, prone to sleepless nights in the highways and byways of the world; hungry, for we have only eaten at places where doors did not slam in our faces. Some doors opened into cozy working homes and the food was the same as the people in the house ate. It satisfied. At other places, refuse was handed to us. That was not good and left us sick. Yes, we are beggars for the food of the soul, for the shelter of the heart.

– 33 –

O Jesus, to whom should we come if not to the Prince of Love? For You too, O Lord, are, in a way, a Beggar. You condescend to leave all and come and beg for the love of my heart, my unworthy, little, insignificant heart. For such as it is, it is Yours. O Jesus: Yours, Yours!   (July 3, 1934)

A Free Gift

Dear Lord, make me understand that Your graces are a free gift, not the result of my trying or my goodness. For, at best, I do not deserve any; they are not proportioned to my merits or lack of merits. You must make me understand that love is the guiding star of all those inexplicable actions of Yours on my behalf.

Give me the understanding of Your death for us—for me. You see, I do not seem to grasp that You died of love, for love, through love. I know it is almost impossible for me to understand such love—God dying to save humanity en masse and individually. O Jesus, the mystery is too much for me. But teach me, at least, to accept it on faith.   (July 4, 1934)

Fear

O Jesus, I stand before You again! Help me! What have I to fear, I who profess to be a Christian, Your follower? Humiliations? Ridicule? What of it? Did You not have Your share of them?! O Jesus, You see how weak and unworthy I am. O Lord of my soul, help me.

I refuse to give in to fear of any kind. You are my beginning and end. For You I started; for You I finish. If it is Your will that my work progress, Yours is the glory. If it is Your desire that it stop, Yours is the will. I am prepared to face misery and praise, success and failure alike. For, at best, what can I lose except my life? It is Yours already, for I have no fear of death. It is the direct road to purgatory and to You. O Jesus, my Lord and my God, Your will be done in me now and forever. Amen.
               (July 4, 1934)

Tiredness

Like a gray blanket, tiredness and life in general have settled on me. O Jesus, help me to get up again, to fight the good fight. Bless my efforts and make me strong.

Jesus I love You. Teach me to love You more and more!

(July 18, 1934)

To Know the Father

O Jesus, alone and in daily need, I hunger not for the bread of the body, but for the bread of the soul. I want to be perfect as You and the Father are perfect. I pray for the Holy Spirit, without whom I cannot be strong or comprehend Your mystery. Teach me to know the Father. Teach me, after knowing Him, to trust Him implicitly.

There is so much to do in life for Your sake. Give me the courage to do it.   (July 19, 1934)

Trust in Little Things

O Jesus, lift my heart up above the worries of little things, for they, like grains of dust, have great power. They can stop noble desires and deaden the most ardent hearts. Let me be small and humble; let me be always seeking only Your glory. For what am I? Every little breath I take, I do so by Your grace only. You hold my very life in Your hands. How could I then lack trust in You? Inflame my heart with Your love, the source of all virtue, especially of trust. I love You, O Jesus. Teach me to love You hourly—every minute and second more and more!

(July 20, 1934)

Gratitude

O Jesus, I thank You for men and women who, enlightened by the Holy Spirit, are able to put Your teaching into clear and comprehensible form. I thank You for those who bring You to us through the sacraments, Your Church, their example, their words.

I ask humbly, on my knees, to profit by Your word as explained by them. I ask the Holy Spirit to enlighten my poor intellect so that I can not only comprehend Your teachings but, inflamed with love for You, put them into practice in my daily life, thus worshiping, through You, with the help of the Holy Spirit, our eternal Father in the Holy Trinity.   (July 23, 1934)

Jesus, Help Me to Become a Saint

Jesus, help me to become a saint.

Jesus, help me to help others.

Jesus, help me to overcome myself.

Jesus, help me to understand Your truths.

Jesus, help me to be poor for Your sake.

Jesus, help me to be humble.

Jesus, teach me to conform my will to Yours.

Jesus, teach me to be charitable.

Jesus, give me purity of intention.

Jesus, inflame my heart with love of You.

I resolve to apply myself to the study of Jesus, to imitate him and thus become a saint.   (July 23, 1934)

The Power of Sanctity

O Jesus, make me realize the power of sanctity, the indwelling of the Holy Trinity in the pure soul, the possession by the devil of an indecent one.

Let me realize the immensity of Your love and answer the only answer I will give to it: "Jesus, make me a saint!"

(July 24, 1934)

O Jesus, Be My Light!

Shine in my soul that I might see its very darkest corners and do penance for my sins. Give me light to see in the darkness of this world. O Jesus, You see my heart. I love You; I firmly believe in You and in Your Church. But look at my life! Seemingly I spend it doing good to others; how short this falls of what I could do if I cooperated with all Your graces.

O Jesus, I know one thing. I love You. I want to serve You more and more. For faith without works is dead. But I am so weak, and temptations so strong. I can do nothing, be it even for a moment, a second, without You.

Be my light! Shine in my soul even when it seems heavy and tired—when prayers, mortifications and all things of light are distasteful to me, when I yearn for the "peace" of darkness, forgetting that there is no peace in it, nothing but sin. O Jesus, make me strong in the light of Your faith, that overcoming the weariness and temptation of the flesh, I might walk in Your light only, and always. (July 25, 1934)

Give Me Your Light

O Holy Spirit, give me Your light. Help me to acquire Your spirit of love. Move my little puny intellect into Your service, into the light. Keep me from darkness. Keep me from sin, which is absolute darkness. Inspire me! Grant me Your supreme gift of prayer for perseverance, understanding, and fortitude. You are the power of Christ, the love of His Father. Be You my light that I might never walk in the shadows but see things in their right value, seek that which is most precious: the Kingdom of God.

O Holy Spirit, I adore and love You. Help me to become a saint. (July 26, 1934)

Teach Me to Pray

Holy Spirit and Jesus Christ, My Lord, teach me to pray—to worship, adore, petition, and thank my Father who is in Heaven. You have given me a prayer that is all mine as a Christian—the Our Father. Give me the grace to say it sweetly, to meditate on it, to live it. Give me the gift of prayer.

Release the weariness of my spirit imprisoned in a tired body. The spirit is willing, O Lord, but the flesh is weak. Teach me to pray, O Jesus, You who prayed so much. Teach me also that my prayer cannot be selfish, for it is a Christian prayer. Let it include the world, O Jesus. Let it bring me closer to You. Teach me to pray. Give me, Your humble servant, the gift of prayer that I might glorify Our Father, "who art in heaven."

(July 27, 1934)

Forgive My Indifference, Lord

O Jesus, my Lord, forgive me my indifference and emptiness, my strange indifference to Your presence in the Blessed Sacrament. You are there for me to come and worship daily. And how often do I enter a Catholic Church for Mass and Communion tired, miserable, and distracted—believing, yet somehow taking it all for granted! My visits—short and so inadequate! Jesus, I ask earnestly for the gift to love You, and loving You, to understand the tremendous mystery of my glorious faith!

My Lord and my God is mine; He is with me in the Blessed Sacrament. I can receive Him daily, visit Him, make Him my closest friend and associate in all my daily life.

O Jesus, let this mystery penetrate every fiber of my being, every inch of my mind, my heart, my soul. Let me act accordingly that my life, united to You, may become an eternal sacrifice.

O Jesus, I love You. Make me love You more and more!

(July 28, 1934)

How Shall I Serve You, Lord?

Jesus, my Lord and my God! To love You, to serve You has always been my dream, my desire, my goal. But so many times have I been perturbed by the world's applause, or discouraged by the world's blame that I forgot that it was You I wanted to serve.

O Jesus of Nazareth, Son of Man, my God, I see again it matters not: activity, repose, blame or applause, as You will. It all comes from You and goes back to You, my Beloved.

So make me bold to catch the souls of men and women for You. Make me humble to bring them to You. Make me active to will them to You. Give me inactivity to pray for them. Make me understand that whatever I do for love of You is Yours, as I am Yours. Let all my life be one glad lifting up of my heart to You—all for the glory of God! (July 29, 1934)

To Love You More

O Jesus, You are love! I know it. I feel it. The answer is in my heart. I love You with, it seems, but one wish: to love You more and more.

Jesus, why is this heart of mine so restless? Why, having given You three quarters, do I hesitate so much to give You all? O Jesus of Nazareth, why? I am so simple, so unworthy. Help me. For although I do not understand the whys and wherefores of it all, I am ready, O Jesus, to follow You anywhere to the end! (August 6, 1934)

Make Me Prayerful

O Jesus, my Lord and my God! Teach me to pray humbly, simply. Teach me to come to You for everything. Teach me to ask You for the smallest things in life—and the biggest. Teach me to do all things with prayer. Teach me to realize that prayers are manifold; that just as speaking to You is prayer, listening to You is prayer also. Working for You is prayer in action. Doing nothing, if such is Your will, is also prayer. Pain and sorrow, born patiently, are also praying.

Teach me, O Son of Man, the power, the glory, the need for prayer. Make me prayerful. Remind me especially to pray in time of temptation, not to give up praying in time of indifference and desolation. Jesus, make my whole life a prayer to You.

(August 8, 1934)

The Joy of the Cross Is Love

Jesus, today I want to just think of You without books or prayers, just to consider Your life and what it means to me. You are Love. Religion is really loving You. And in that love all is told: mortification, prayers, self–denial. All becomes easy, based on love.

Jesus, I love You. All I do, You know, is neither from fear of hell nor desire for heaven. It is just out of love for You, my God and my Savior.

Please do not allow me to take any glory in praise. Let me work more, yet even more, for You alone, never looking for gratitude, never expecting a reward here on earth.

Jesus, be my beginning and end each day!

(August 9, 1934)

My Love Is Here

Dear Jesus, today at Communion was bliss. I felt Your presence so profoundly! O Lord of heaven and earth! Prostrate before You, I adore You. What can I say! My Lord and my God is in my soul! O Jesus, I believe with all my heart and my soul that You are Christ Our Lord, the Second Person of the Holy Trinity, come down to save us from sin. I believe this even unto death.

How can I thank You, for how can nothingness thank the infinite? I ask only for purity of intention, for a love forever growing, for more courage to put this love into deeds on Your behalf. O Jesus, I love You. Teach me to burn with love, consuming myself for it. (August 11, 1934)

Your Will

Jesus, teach me to seek in all things only Your will! Teach me never to deviate from it. O Lord of my heart, always Your will, not mine, be done! (August 13, 1934)

My Heart's Desire

O, may I love You more and always more! Teach my heart to find You everywhere. Teach my soul Your beauty, to explore and fly to You upon the wings of prayer.

O most fair, whom I have never seen; most true, whose voice in time I have not heard, who are and shall ever be, and who have been unceasingly.

O eternal Word, grant my heart a knowledge of the good, and to my mind the gift of light to see. For love by love alone is understood, and truth is only known when known in You. So may my intellect contemplate You until my heart falls prostrate before You!

O Jesus, my very own! Here is summed up my heart's desire: to love You, ever more and more, until I can no longer live, and die from Love! And let this love be not only of the mind and heart. Let it go forth and heal and help. Let it be found in the harvest of souls brought back to Your sacred fold!

(August 20, 1934)

The Gift I Seek

O Jesus, prostrate before You, I beg only for one gift: an all-consuming love of You, a supernatural love of You, an all-enhancing love of You, a gentle love of You, a childlike love of You, a love of You until death, a love of You unafraid of martyrdom, a love of all the poor in You, a love of all the sick in You, a love of all the strayed ones in You, a love of all the sorrowful ones in You, a love of all the lonely ones in You, a love of all the tired ones in You, a love of all the little ones in You, a love of all the scoffing ones in You, a love of all sinners in You.

O Jesus, my prayer is: make me love You more and more, and love everyone in You! (August 20, 1934)

Let Not the Joys of the Earth Dim Your Face

O Jesus, let not the cry of friendships make me deaf to Your quiet voice. Let not human love uproot my love for You. O Jesus, I love You. I want to love You more and more, yet I am afraid just now of being unfaithful to You. Holy Spirit, my protector, be with me. Blessed Virgin, leave me not.

(August 28, 1934)

Show Me the Way

Dear Jesus, show me the way. Alone and weary I stand under the weight of my sins! Jesus, my Lord, prostrate before You, I beg Your forgiveness! Never have I realized my sinfulness as vividly as I do now, when I see so many good, holy people around me.

O Jesus, have mercy on me. Mary, pray for me. Dear St. Catherine, pray for me. Angel Guardian, pray for me.

(September 2, 1934)

Give Me Grace

O Jesus, give me strength and grace to do the things I must without counting the cost. Give me grace to do all for You. You know how I love You, yet You see how weak I am in the face of temptation. O Jesus, help me to help others and help myself. I love You. Make me love You more and more.

(September 6, 1934)

An Ocean of Work

I am embarking on a great ocean of work for You, Beloved. It looks so big. It looks so forbidding, so impossible, this task of mine. Yet all is simple to those of faith and at Your feet I put all my works. At Your feet I put all my prayers. Bless them; let them prosper if it is Your will. Use me, Jesus, as You will for the good of others. Have pity on the hungry multitude.

(September 7, 1934)

For a Love of Poverty

Jesus, teach me that inner love of poverty which values not the things of the world. Detach my heart from earthly possessions, first physical, then even those of the heart. Let me lose myself in You, want nothing but You, work for nothing but to bring souls to You. And, if such is Your will, let me give up all I possess for You.

(October 18, 1934)

Lift Up My Heart

"And I, when I am lifted up, will draw all things to myself."
(*Jn 12:32*)

O Jesus, how beautiful is Your word; like a fresh, cool fountain of water, it falls on our parched hearts.

O Jesus, all-wise God, You came down to be lifted up—from humility, pain, agony—all for love.

Lift my heart up, too, so it might see the sorrow of humanity and be ready to participate in Your suffering for them. Lift my heart up so it might realize more the need of the world and run to fill it. Lift my heart up so that it should see the world's thirst for truth and try to quench it. Lift my heart up to Yours so mine should forever hide in Yours and catch fire from Yours and never waver or stop or hesitate when the work is Yours and there is a soul to save.

Give me love, Your love, and then send me into the midst of Your battle.

I am ready, Lord. In You I can do all things!

(October 19, 1934)

The Road of Leadership

Jesus, You have opened before me the road of leadership, loneliness, and sorrows. You know Yourself how absolutely unworthy I am, Beloved. But in all things of my life, Your will is the only compass. If You so desire, here I am. Do with me what You will. Only give me the grace to persevere.

I know I will falter and fall, stumble and stop. But You will be at my side—won't You Dearest?—and all will be well.

Give me patience. Give me understanding. Above all, give me love to be patient and quiet and humble under it all.

(October 25, 1934)

Death

Dear Lord, as the years go on I begin to realize the beauty and terrible joy of death. It is the opening of a door to You; it is the return home.

O Jesus, I accept any death You have prepared for me and offer its agony for the one seemingly impossible cause of converting and straightening out the world.

(November 7, 1934)

How Unfit I Am

It is a long time since I have written here. Yet my thoughts have never been far from You, O Lord, as You so well know. But looking back over these months, I see again how little fitted I am to be Your friend and work for You, Beloved. I am impatient, irritable, a slave of habits, cross, a bad mother, a bad teacher, a bad boss, exaggerating for the sake of effect, preaching and not practicing. How is that for a picture? Especially if You add this: always tired, always longing for privacy, always wanting normal life without any spiritual problems—mine or others—to face. O Jesus, help me, help me, for You alone can have hope of improving material like that!

Beloved of my heart, there is only one thing necessary for me, and that is Your love which, in turn, can make me love You. To do all things because of love, not out of desire for reward or fear of punishment—just love, love, love, and purity of intention; to just do things out of pure love for Your glory!

O Jesus, what a bliss it would be, Beloved. I thank You, though, for all the trials of the past month—the indifference of people, the trials of mind, the irritations of working with others, the one thousand difficulties I have to face daily. Give me Your grace to love You, and I will begin over and over again.

Beloved Jesus, I love You! Teach me to love You more and more!

(December 6?, 1934)

Doing and Being

Lord, just now, with the feast of the Birth approaching, I ask myself: "What am I? What have I done?" A year has passed. I do not know if I shall live the next. If I were to die, what would I have been? What would I have done?

In the line of "doing," all seems outwardly well. I have fulfilled the precepts of corporal and some spiritual works of mercy. But inwardly, has my "doing" been pure, has my intention been pure also?

Here I touch on what I am. O Jesus, have mercy on me a sinner! Open my eyes that I might see, my ears that I might hear, my intelligence that I might understand and, above all, my will that I might follow!

In a few days, I shall kneel at Your crib. I shall behold the miracle of miracles: absolute power, helpless; the Creator in the arms of a creature; Love in a tangible form.

It is the time of gifts. I ask for one and only one: the gift of love. Jesus, my Lord, my God, my friend and my beloved, I ask for love of You. I offer You my heart to be pierced by the flame of Divine Love. I want to live only to increase in love for You and to be able to prove that love to You by serving and loving Your little ones, the poor.

O Jesus, blend in me the "being" and the "doing," at Your convenience, at Your desire, so when You look at me, I shall not be distasteful to Your eyes!

Next year, I want to concentrate on "being." Teach me, O Jesus, to understand the truth that alone we are nothing; that You, working through us, can save the world. But in order for You to work through us, we must be fit for Your touch. Teach me to be fit. Show me the way of prayer, mortification and zeal, obedience and love.

Jesus, I love You. Teach me to love You more and more. Amen.   (December 21, 1934)

Faith

Dear Jesus, faith is the invincible shield of a Christian's life. In it, he is secure from the world. With it, he is powerful as a giant. In it, he can do all things.

Give me faith, O Lord. I believe. Help my unbelief. Let my faith be a candle, lighted and straight, burning itself out in good works, without which faith is dead. O Jesus, help me. For I daily, hourly, every minute need that faith to overcome temptations and myself, and to advance in virtue. Help me, Jesus, for You alone are the root of faith.   (January 9, 1935)

Not Initiative but Acceptance

Dear Jesus, for long I thought that by using my ingenuity, by urging myself on, I could do better than You Yourself could do and surpass Your desires. I thought—it is always the same illusion—that the work of sanctity was an enterprise before being an acceptance; that it was a personal initiative before being a respectful answer; that it was for me to begin the great work! Whereas my first act should be thanking You for having already begun it in me by Your grace, forestalling all my desire.

(January 10, 1935)

Conformity to God's Will

Dear Jesus, as I read of the perfect conformity of St. Francis' will with Yours, I marvel. It seems so hard to submit in illness, difficulties, calumnies. Yet with all my mind, heart and soul, I want to. I know it is the only way to You.

In my life, my great cross is the dislike of, misunderstandings with, and at times, calumnies and persecutions from people. Dear Jesus, You know how profoundly they wound me when I am faced with them. Yet I realize they are stepping stones to You. May I then offer to You these difficulties in reparation for the times when I have rebelled against Your will. And I repeat, as I do daily, give me the gift—at every time and in all things—of conforming my will to Yours.

(January 12, 1935)

On Being an Example

Dear Jesus, enlighten my understanding to realize that the first step to the salvation of others is example. For one who is following Your footsteps will keep his soul before Your face.

And it is the glory of Your face reflected in him that will work the example.

O Jesus, make me realize this yet more vividly, for it seems I never shall be able to understand it fully. How far from fulfilling Your precepts I am! Look at me, after years of Your love, Your grace, Your help! I'm still the same proud, sinful, erring, slothful, sensual person. It seems I have not started on the right road, even now.

Yet whatever my faults, I shall never doubt Your mercy. On it, I throw myself. In it, I hide. For in it alone lies my salvation. I believe and trust in You with all my faculties.

O Jesus, have mercy on me a sinner! I will never remain lying in the mire, no matter how deeply I fall. I shall get up at once. And, trusting and repentant, start again and again. For in You alone is life!

Teach me, help me to lead others to You by example. Help me to help others as well as myself. St. Francis, beloved of Christ, be at my side. (January 13, 1935)

Absolute Trust

Dearest Lord, how can I speak to You? My growing knowledge of myself in the eyes of others is a staggering revelation. I did not quite realize what I was like, but now I do know. The picture is really black, Jesus. And the thought that this is what I bring to You is crushing! Shall I never improve, never correspond to Your grace? What You have done for me and what I am, O Jesus! Have mercy on me, a sinner.

Do not let me lose hope, O Beloved, as I am so inclined to do when I hear criticisms heaped on me as so many coals on the fire. Help me, O Jesus, to love the criticisms, to be profoundly grateful to those who express them, for they are my teachers, and often, I am all that they say I am. Make me meek and humble. Help me, Jesus. Teach me to bear it all as a Franciscan should. Teach me to love it. Teach me to add patience and forbearance to love. (January 21, 1935)

Give Me Purity of Mind, Heart and Body

Purity is a wonderful virtue. Temptations against it are terrible, especially for lay men and women. Help me, who all my life have been exposed to them. Help me to overcome them, and in order to overcome them, to overcome myself.

Teach me, O Jesus, to do so. You know how much I stand in need of it! Help me to understand. As each year goes by, I seem to see and understand more and more. It is as if a veil is lifting slowly from my mind. Help me, O Jesus, to act according to this always-new understanding. (January 30, 1935)

You Are My Guide

Dearest Lord, there is, in my heart, such a desire to serve You, such a love for my poor brothers and sisters, such a desire to bring them back to You! But it seems I always stop short of action. Or, when I act, my motives are so mixed that I wonder if they are pleasing to You.

I have no immediate superiors to obey—only my confessors and those I work for, who give me such big latitudes. It is to You and Your Word that I must look for guidance. In all things I trust and conform my will to Yours, O Jesus.

O Jesus, You are all wise. Help me, since You have so willed, to fulfill these heavy duties, with Your grace, to the best of my ability. O Beloved, teach me. Make me a saint. Do not spare me in the making! I love You. Teach me in Your love to find strength, O Jesus! (February 3, 1935)

The Fire of Your Love

Once more, Beloved, in my heart are the fires of love that lift me up. I so desire to please You and serve You well. Again, I have to thank You for this interior grace of spirit and zeal.

Why, oh why, are You so good to me, Beloved, when I least of all deserve it? How many resolutions have I not formed? How many decisions have I not made—always to break them?

But I will never despair of Your mercy as I despair of my own wickedness. O Jesus, help me! Without Your help I am weak and unable to stand up. But with Your help, O Jesus, I propose once more to reform my life. Help me, O Lord, to be gentle always. Teach me to really see You in all people.

(February 4, 1935)

The Beginning of Love

Mortification seems to be the one thing I really shirk. It is so hard a thing, yet so necessary.

Jesus, teach me the beginning of love: sacrifice. For if anyone needs it, I do. I am so sinful. Let me start today and mortify my senses, in a hidden way.

I will start with little things: refusals of second helpings, and of dainty food and so forth. Especially, teach me to accept those mortifications of spirit You send me with joy.

(February 5, 1935)

Mortification

Mortification is a virtue so necessary to offset the devil. O Jesus, I, who am never, it seems, capable of mortifications, should ponder within my soul the need for them more than anyone else. To have to organize and lead others calls for a very mortified person. How unworthy I am of the grace of God!

Jesus teach me the need for mortifications. Then give me the strength to carry them out. (February 6, 1935)

Simplicity

Simplicity is a virtue hard to acquire, I know. Without the grace of God, it is impossible. Help me to be simple of faith, simple of devotion, open and simple in my speech—never hiding thoughts in my heart. The simple are light of heart. Give me that lightness so my service will be more acceptable to You.

(February 8, 1935)

First Steps

How little as yet do I realize the realities of the spiritual life, O my Lord and my God! I am like a little child just let out of swaddling clothes who tries vainly to stand on its feet. Only the gentle hands of its mother can help a child with those first steps. Realizing this, O Jesus, I throw myself into the loving, gentle arms of Your love, grace and mercy—truly realizing that alone I can do nothing.

Help me, O Beloved Master. Teach me the first steps of spiritual walking. Help me to grow in holiness under Your guidance. Make me a saint. Do not spare me in the making. O Jesus, God of my heart! (February 10, 1935)

Lord, I Am Not Worthy

O Jesus, today I just want to talk to You like a child to its mother, like a friend to a friend, like a servant to his master!

Beloved, why have You chosen me for this work? I know You desire to show Your glory to the least worthy people! But how can any light shine through a dark vessel?

Look at me—lazy, proud, full of self-satisfaction, irritable, talkative, foolish, untruthful! Have mercy on me. If it is Your wish, I submit to it. But, O Lord, cleanse me, allowing at least a little bit of Your light to shine to others through me for I'm not helping them, but only hindering them. Jesus of Nazareth, bless Your unworthy servant.

I neither understand authority nor wield it well. Have pity on me. (February 12, 1935)

Priests

My dear Lord, You know how I love and respect the priesthood. Help me to ever grow in this, never to judge a priest, never to criticize one. Help me to see You in each of them. (February 17, 1935)

The Eucharist

O Jesus, what can I say when I contemplate Your graciousness to us in the Blessed Sacrament: God, always waiting for His people! I ask You one thing—to love You, to understand the beauty of the Eucharist, to spread Eucharistic devotion. O Jesus, O Mary, have pity on me a sinner.

(February 19, 1935)

To Sow

My dear Lord, my sole endeavor is to sow and sow deep; to not look behind to see whether it sends up shoots; to take thought only to sow with all my mind, with all my heart; to take no account of the harvest, for harvesting is no account of mine.

(February 20, 1935)

The Passion of Christ

Dear Jesus, You know I love to meditate on Your Passion because it gives me hope. As I look upon myself—vain, miserable hypocrite that I am—I lose hope. When my eyes light on a crucifix I weep, and feel that such love as this begets hope. I try again!

Dearest Lord, only Your love could stand such eternal starts all over again! Prostrate before Your cross in spirit, I moan and weep for my lack of love.

O Jesus, have mercy on me, a sinner. Inflame my heart with such love that it will burn away all stain of sin, working only for You, through You, and by You. I love You. Make me love You more and more, O Jesus! Help of the weak, have pity on me. All for Your glory!

(February 21, 1935)

Father

Father, it is hard for me to realize Your presence. Yet I know You are here. And I know You so loved the world as to give Your Son to it. The profound debt we owed could only have been paid by Christ!

Father, I thank You for the coming of Your Son. I run to You in my prayers, asking for my needs daily. Give me the grace to be like a little child before You, trusting and obedient to Your will. (February 27, 1935)

The Loneliness of Christ

Dear Lord, what a consolation are meditations on Your Passion. What profound lessons one can draw from them. What an example to follow as I go about Your work day by day. I, too, often feel prevented from doing my work because of human jealousies, criticisms, dislikes, petty little things that loom large in my little sphere. Yet why should I, Your most humble servant, fare better than You, my Master, in Your utter loneliness and desolation? Why should I desire comfort and friends?

Loneliness for us mortals is hard to bear. Yet You came to earth to show us the way. The desert, the Garden of Olives, Gethsemane, the Way of the Cross, Calvary, all point to Your loneliness.

So I will accept walking alone for Your sake, remembering that I did not start out for people but for You, Beloved! O Jesus, I am weak. Help me! Do not allow me to stop any of Your work because of human respect. All for You, no matter what comes. All for You, if it is Your will. (February 28, 1935)

Free Will

Beloved, I contemplate Your great love for us, Your desire to save all souls, Your untiring efforts, Your utter forgetfulness of Yourself, Your opening of the gates of heaven, Your very death on the cross—all the outpouring of Your divine love. Yet I see You did not force humanity to love You. We have free will. We can choose to reject Your love. We can deliberately prevent the effect of Your grace in our souls.

Through the centuries, thousands of men and women will reject You. Some will even try to kill You in the souls of others.

Beloved, I am a great sinner, but I cannot stand indifferently watching this perversion, this destruction of You in the hearts and souls of countless multitudes. Here I am, O Lord, the humblest, the worst servant chosen to go and work in Your vineyard. I do not ask the honorable tasks. I only ask the hardest, the most thankless, the hidden ones.

Jesus, I love You. Help me to show this love by bringing others to You. Your cry, "I am thirsty,"[7] is before me daily. I ask that You know only this: I love You. I want to console You. I want to bring men and women to You, and to begin with, I want to bring myself. (March 3, 1935)

Turning Evil into Good

Beloved, last week was a very hard one. My heart is heavy with pain! All I want to do is bring men and women to You. But somehow, with those who have come to help me, I feel sorrowful, for their minds are not on Your glory, Beloved. Gossip and dissension are rife.

So many times in Your lifetime You turned evil into good. O Jesus, Beloved, do not leave me now. Without You, all is ashes; all is bitter. I love You. Teach me to love You more and more. Give me fortitude, peace, love of You, faith and trust to carry on! (March 4, 1935)

The Mocking of Christ

Your Passion! I love meditating on Your Passion, for although my intellect will never absorb the immensity of the sacrifice, my heart seems daily to see more and understand more. Daily, I desire a little more to be like You. Daily I pray for a better life. Daily, I seem to have a little more courage, for it comes from merely thinking of You, Beloved! How You suffered—the mocking, the bodily pain; how deeply they must have wounded You. For Your soul, Your body, were so supremely sensitive.

O Jesus, I want to share in Your suffering, to bring humanity—even one person—to its senses. I feel so unhappy when I behold the world. It is as if You never existed!

Beloved, give me a heart of fire which will serve and love Your little ones! O Jesus, I love You. (March 6, 1935)

I Weep at the Thought of Your Loneliness

Beloved, as I see You hanging from the cross, my heart feels sad unto death. Often I have wept at the thought of Your loneliness. Only three were with You—three out of the multitudes to whom You had done good, to whom You had taught the words of eternal life! Three!

Jesus, my Lord and my God, forgive my absence; forgive it. Allow me to stay with You at the foot of the cross always, to console You by trying to be a saint. Help me in this. I want to be a saint for You because You told us to. I love You and ask to love You more and more, forevermore, until my heart is a blazing furnace of love lighting other souls. (March 7, 1935)

Forgiveness

Beloved, my heart is torn by sorrow. I love You. I want to serve You. But human beings tear my heart to pieces. Give me strength, humility, understanding. Above all, give me forgiveness—never to hold a grudge against anyone, to love all alike. O Jesus, please! I do want to serve You in humility. Give me love of Yourself, humility, purity of intention, the gift of prayer. O Beloved, I will besiege You for these gifts for they will bring me nearer to You. (March 8, 1935)

Let Me Make Up for Those Who Hurt You

They laughed at You, Beloved, and jeered. Amidst jokes and ribaldry, they crucified You. Daily I hear this laughter. Daily I see this ribaldry of the people who have forgotten their God! Beloved, allow me to make up for it. Give me the desire, give me the grace, and again, the strength to go on and make reparation for others.

These are the little things I can do and will try to do for this end, Beloved:

1) Attend an extra Mass when I can, at noon, to make up for Catholics who do not go on Sunday.

2) Offer little, hidden mortifications of food for those who do not fast or make penance.

3) Give up smoking on Sundays and during Lent.

4) Make the Way of the Cross daily in reparation for my sins and the world's.

5) Make the Way of the Cross on Sundays for atheists.

6) Cultivate silence in answer to provocation; offer it up for victims of social injustice.

7) Be patient at all times to soften the hearts of greedy and selfish employers.

8) Offer incessant prayers for the right spirit.

(March 10, 1935)

From Light to Darkness

O Beloved, it is hard! Life brings so many irritating, tragic things. Look at today—right after prayer and Communion—everything seems black and dark again, broken and lost. Jesus, Jesus, do not leave me. I am afraid! Beloved, I cannot stand up alone. I love You. I love You. I love You! My heart goes out to You. I want to be Your servant, and the next moment, my body positively shakes with anger. How can it be, Beloved? Help me!

(March 11, 1935)

The Cross of Little Things

O Jesus, as I stand before You my sins rise and confront me. I feel like weeping. Beloved, if it were not for Your grace giving me faith and confidence in Your eternal goodness, justice, and mercy, I could not stand it.

I seem to be crucified on the cross of little things. Vainly do I promise bigger ones at the foot of Your altar; little things hold me fast. In all I see Your will, Beloved. Perhaps little things are big to me. Teach me! Teach me! Help me! Help me! Help me to overcome this insane irritability which surges like so many waves every second of my life. Jesus I speak to You of all these insignificant things because I have no one else to speak to about them. Beloved, help me. (March 12, 1935)

Hide Me in Your Heart

Beloved, do not leave me alone. As it is, my loneliness is so intense. Around me are people who do not understand me, who misunderstand me all the time, criticize in season and out of season. Somehow this loneliness is worse because I am in a crowd. Never any privacy, never any respite from it all. And then, temptation.

O Beloved, hide me in Your heart. Do not let me go. The thought of a husband-lover, of a quiet heart, of not having to earn money, of long nights of love and peace and sleep—a human heart that really cares! I know all this is not for me. Yet the picture raises itself daily at times and beckons like a fairyland.

What have I to offer You, Beloved! Broken years of struggles and falls, a desert of loneliness, a heart broken by ingratitude, rusty, earth-covered talents that I, too, foolishly bury in the earth of time against Your call.[8]

Beloved, have pity on me. Do not remove my cross. I love it as I love You. Just be my Cyrene. Help me to carry it a little while. Let me put my weary head on Your sacred feet. Let me kiss them daily as Magdalene kissed them. Let me rest with You awhile. I am tired, tired of the wickedness, the selfishness of others and my own! (March 13, 1935)

Make My Love a Bonfire

Beloved, never allow me to stray from You. How often have I asked this, and how often have I broken it! There is, in my soul, a great desire for love of You, an immense desire to bring people to You, an overwhelming need to live for You, in You, with You. All things that are not Yours are bitter to me. Yet I stray away from You. How is it, Beloved? How can it be? Help me. Make me a saint in spite of myself.

Dimly I see. Gropingly I crawl in the right direction. Daily, it seems to me, I advance a little toward light. Then comes darkness again. Beloved, do not leave me alone too long to languish in sorrow.

I love You. It is like a fire in my heart, driving me joyfully to do more and more for You, Beloved. Blow that fire into a great bonfire, which will draw to You men and women, people for whom You have given Your love and for whom You are in the Blessed Sacrament.

Make me a saint so I might love You more. For saints do, don't they? I want to love You as they do, Beloved, unto death itself! (March 14, 1935)

Christian Perfection

"For myself, I know of no Christian perfection other than to love God with our whole heart and our neighbor as ourselves." (St. Francis de Sales)

This is the way I feel, Beloved! It seems I have an urge in the depth of my heart to go and help the souls and bodies of others. Life in the fashionable world bores me. All conversations seem trite except ones about You or in You. I am truly happy only when I am about Your business.

It is so simple, Lord. You said, "Whatsoever you do to the least of my brothers, you do to me."[9] Well, how can I rest when I know and see so many Christs walking in misery?

I love Your Passion. To me it is an eternal renewal of the greatest marvel of love! God came down for love of men and women! What greater mystery is there in life, even after life? None that I know of. It seems absolutely extraordinary to forget about it.

But the worldly forget. And daily, hourly, minute by minute, they renew Your Passion in Your poor! O Beloved, one does not have to go to church to make the Way of the Cross. All one has to do is walk the high and low ways of the world. Everywhere—in shops, factories, homes, streets—You walk the road to Calvary in the poor!

At moments, it seems to me I am surrounded with a sea, a forest, of crosses. On each is crucified "another Christ." How, then, can I rest in peace? How can I be indifferent? O Beloved, I must come, sinful and unworthy as I am, and help them—here be a Cyrene, there a Veronica. Further on bring fresh water to the parched lips of men and women. Here help children. The works are many and glorious.

Yes, I love You, yet I want to love You more.

(March 16, 1935)

For Tears for My Sins

Prostrate at Your feet, I again implore You for this supreme gift, an all-consuming love for You. Let that love be a furnace of fire. Let it burn out all sins from my soul, leaving only my tears to be shed for them.

For You see, my Lord, I have as yet, it seems to me, little realization of my sins. I confess them. I feel sorry, profoundly so, at the time; then I forget about them as if they never have been, trusting completely to the ocean of Your Divine Mercy, trying to start the day afresh. Am I right?

I read in so many holy books that Your great lovers wept over their slightest imperfections! Teach me sorrow for my sin, Beloved. I would cheerfully die for You. And, yet, look at me! How sensitive to criticism I am! How I consider human respect! O Beloved, let my love for You overcome it all. I ask to love You more, ever more, because love is stronger than anything in the world, stronger than death!

I love all those of Your saints who loved You well: St. Francis Xavier, St. Francis of Assisi. Simply and fearlessly, they trusted in You and went ahead in whatever You had prepared for them to do. So shall I, Beloved! I give all of myself to You. I do not want to keep anything back. If You desire any friendship I have, it is Yours too, Beloved. I want to surrender all to You and only concern myself with Your work, Your desires, Your wishes! I thank You for the light that You have already given me. I will go on doing what I am doing to the best of my ability, trusting You completely.

I leave all things in Your hands, my God and my Lord. Do with me as You want! Help me to do Your will. Above all, give me Your love and inflame my heart with love for You. Help me to bring men and women to You. Give me light to understand better the mysteries of Your love—Your Incarnation, Eucharist, and Passion.

Give me the gift of prayer. Holy Spirit, Beloved Spirit of my heart, make my intellect Your abode so that always submissive to Your light, I may direct my will accordingly. Blessed Mother of God, give me the gift of increased devotion to You for You are the channel of all grace! Help me to love Your Son as You have loved Him. I ask to share with Him His dark day, when He was alone! Help me, Mother of Christ, to be faithful unto the end! (March 16, 1935)

Horror for Sin

My Lord and my God, I have asked You for new light and You have given it to me. I have never before realized what an outrage sin is to Your majesty. I honestly thought only of Your mercy in forgiving it or of Your three falls on the way to Calvary, when You gave us the lesson to rise at once when we fall. So I try to do. But now I will try to absorb this new thought: horror for sin. (March 16, 1935)

What a Solace This Is!

Deep down in my heart today there is peace. Lord of my heart, I thank You for it. These moments of respite in the daily warfare are like an oasis in an arid desert. To You, O Jesus, I can speak of all things; to You I can come with all my sorrows and joys. What a solace this is, Beloved.

The world has forgotten You. It falls to us who love You to do Your work. It is our place and duty to reawaken in their hearts Your love and the knowledge of You. Jesus, Beloved of my soul, help me to do this. For I love You, I love You, I love You. Again and again and again I thank You for Your graces.

(March 18, 1935)

Sin Is Worse than Death

"Sin is worse than death." How many times have I heard this statement, never paying much attention to it. The day before yesterday sin in all its ugliness suddenly appeared before me. Strange, a human being can live a lifetime and not realize the full deadliness of sin! (March 18, 1935)

The Thought of the Trinity Frightens Me

Yesterday I read a book by a holy priest, Fr. Raoul Plus, about *God Within Us*. He spoke beautifully about Your indwelling in us.

Will You forgive me if I speak of You? I love and I adore the Father, the Holy Spirit, and You. But, together, the thought of the Trinity frightens me. In awe and in silence I believe and adore.

Jesus, do You really abide in me? I feel the Church teaches it. I believe it, and yet it is such a miracle, such a stupendous miracle! "My Beloved to me and I to Him." O Jesus, my Lord and my God, since it is so, help me to cleanse my soul. Help me at the slightest venial sin to remember that my heart is the abode of my God!

Beloved, I love You! Daily, I discover new beauty about You. Daily, I find Your love greater, ever merciful. Why then am I not, daily, better and better? Beloved, help me, for there is so little time left! (March 19, 1935)

I Lift My Soul!

"To You, O Lord, I have lifted up my soul!" (*Ps 25:1*)

It is so lovely to be all Yours. To give every moment of my days to You, to work and rest in You, Beloved of my soul. I have loved the glories of Your house, Jesus, my Lord and God. I have put all my trust in You. The little things, the big things, the spiritual and material things, are all Yours. All that we need, all that we are, are Yours. (March 20, 1935)

My Only Refuge Is You

I lift my heart up to You, my soul I give to You. I love You and I implore You to forgive me. Jesus, plead with Your Father in heaven on my behalf. For I have sinned exceedingly. When I contemplate my sin, I would like to run from Your face. But there is nowhere to go because You are everywhere. My only refuge is You—in Your Sacred Heart with its love and mercy, in Your sacred humanity in the Blessed Sacrament with its helpfulness and understanding! O Beloved, I run to You as a child runs to its mother to tell You I am sorry.

Jesus, have mercy on me a sinner. (March 21, 1935)

The Pain of Gossip

"O Lord, deliver my soul from wicked lips and a deceitful tongue." (*Ps 120:2*)

Beloved, I have suffered so much from wicked lips and deceitful tongues. Criticized, distracted, hurt, wounded, I do not know where to lay my heart except at Your feet. Am I hurt to the point of giving up? If yes, then I know at once what I must do: go on! (March 22, 1935)

The Prayer of a Poor Person

"Look upon me, for I am lonely and poor." (*Ps 86:1*)

Dearest Jesus, look upon me for I am lonely and poor—poor in virtue, in willpower, in any gifts I could bring to You; poor in my love for You, so spasmodic, so temperamental; poor in patience; poor in understanding. Jesus, Beloved Jesus, help me to become richer.

I am lonely because I evidently have not yet understood what it means to refrain from serving two masters. I want to be all Yours. Yet the world holds out its allure and I want to get some of it. And miss both.

Also, You know how hopelessly tactless I am about people. I sort of just get their goat up and do not get anywhere with them. Indeed, I am lonely and poor.

O Beloved, help me. (March 25, 1935)

Jesus, Help Me to Clean My Heart

Jesus, why is it I just cannot be good? I pray. I approach the sacraments. I make resolutions and again I fall down. Irritability, impatience, lack of kindness, of understanding, a sharp biting tongue: these things are always with me, Beloved, no matter how I fight. And that's not to speak of the big temptations and habits I must fight—smoking and so forth.

Confronted with this mountain of defects, I weep and almost give up, but then I remember: You sing in my heart. I am compelling You to live in this disorder and these complaints! I begin to try and clean my heart of all superfluous, wicked and unnecessary things, only to be defeated again and again by their tenacity, by the long roots they have taken, by their horrible odor.

O Jesus, Son of Man, forgive me and help me to clean my heart for You. Alone, I shall never do it. But with You, I will!

(March 28, 1935)

I Will Give Praise

Dear Jesus, Beloved Savior, prostrate I fall before You and the Holy Trinity and adore You. How I wish I could tell, explain in words, my love and adoration for You. But words are only empty shells if not followed by action. You said, "If you love me, do the things I taught you."[10]

Beloved, flesh alone cannot perform this; so I beg at Your feet, humbly, for the grace to do it. For I do want to do it with all my soul. It is not easy. Temptations overshadow me everywhere. My temperament is up against it. My humanity rebels against it. But it does not matter. Your grace will suffice, Beloved.

Holy Spirit, be at my side. It is You who help me to fight the spirit of darkness. It is to You that I fly from myself. O Holy Spirit, with the Second Person of the Holy Trinity, abide in my heart, and do not allow me to lose You through sin.

All-seeing and all-loving Father, before You I stand and pray. Forgive my sins through the oblation of Your divine Son, who was born of You, but existed with You, as did the Holy Spirit, forever. I love to think of You, for You are our Father in heaven! Awed by Your majesty, I yet never can forget that I am Your child and Christ is my brother.

O holy and beautiful Trinity, allow me to worship You, and adore, love, and serve You for the sole reason that You are God.

(March 29, 1935)

Jesus, Take All of Me

"But, to me, the judgment of man is but a small thing. He that judges me is the Lord." (St. Bernard)

Jesus, my Lord and my God, grant me the grace not to be influenced by the judgment of others, not to give up, not to rebel against their unjust criticisms, Beloved, but always to remember that I started for You, not for them, that they do not know my intentions. Never let me forget that You are my judge. And, as yesterday, when the hurt is deep, profound and lasting, let me rejoice with You because in Your goodness You have given me the possibility of tasting one thousandth of what You drank of so deeply at Gethsemane: disloyalty, misunderstanding, misinterpretation, and pleasure in hurting You.

O Lord, have mercy on me a sinner! (March 31, 1935)

Give Ear to Me

"O God, hear my prayer. Give ear to the words of my mouth." (*Ps 84:8*)

Beloved, prostrate at Your feet, I contemplate today Your beauty and wisdom, Your Incarnation for love of us, Your great gift of life everlasting! Incredible, it seems to me, to be allowed to love God; impossible to realize that God came down to wrestle that love from the hearts of men and women, and that, until the end of time, He pursues them, a beggar for their love!

Beloved, do I love You enough? I bow my head in shame at this question. Look at me, wanting to love only You, but entangled in worldly affections, in pride, in weakness.

Jesus, Son of Man, have pity on me and on my weakness. See only my burning desire to love You. Hear only my daily cry: "Would that I loved You more, my Lord and my God."

Hear me and grant me Your gift of love, Beloved. Grant me to so love You that I forget the world and remember it only through You. May all my attachments disappear, only to reappear through You. To serve the world's forgotten men and women for You, to love through You and for You, such is my dream. Beloved, I love You. Yesterday, as You know, I was hurt by disloyalty. Today I offer You that hurt in reparation and indulgences for the Holy Souls in purgatory.   (April 1, 1935)

The Sin of Pride

Beloved, at times I can feel Your anger over us. Looking at this world I shudder. Lust we have always had with us, but the sin of this generation is pride. They do not need a God. They are going to destroy You in Your very sacred abode—the hearts of men and women. Your little children are taught to hate You, Beloved, and the earth is shamed.

Look at us: adulterous, selfish, greedy, atheistic. Against all this is Your word and the perfect serenity of heaven, the refuge of the tabernacle.

I am nothing, O Lord, in Your sight, yet I feel the horror of these blasphemies unto the marrow of my bones. Have mercy on us, O Lord; have mercy on us. Stay Your hand. Send grace into these hardened hearts; raise people to atone for their sins. I cannot see any other way, Beloved, but reparation.

You want love, Beloved, and so few give it to You. Allow me to offer this day and all the days of my life in reparation. Beloved, I love You. Teach me to love You more and more, and loving You, serve Your poor more gently and much better than ever before.   (April 2, 1935)

Jesus in Me

"The supernatural life in my soul is the life of Jesus Christ himself, by faith, hope and charity; for Jesus is the meritorious, exemplary, and final cause and, as the Word, with the Father and the Holy Spirit, the efficient cause of sanctifying grace in our souls."[11]

I feel as if I am on the threshold of great discovery. Again and again, my soul has lifted itself up as it has never done before. It is as if my yearning to love You, to be with You, has stretched out my soul as a human being stretches her hands high above her head in supplication.

Glimpses of old truths come to me in most strange moments in a new and sudden way. Walking on the street, I suddenly realize that I carry my own God within me and that, instead of looking for Him elsewhere, all I have to do to feel His presence is to go inward. A happiness and fear enter into me with this. It is as if I should fall and adore my God in my own soul right there and then.

With this realization comes an understanding of the enormity of sin—an understanding which I did not possess until quite recently: sin drives God out of my heart! A creature has the power of evicting its Creator from its soul. But ah, the price of this power is death.

Before this, I stand aghast. My old sins rise to confront me. I fear and tremble, only to realize the infinite mercy of God. Then, like a torrent of joy, comes the thought of God's love—the Incarnation, His hidden life in Nazareth, His three year Apostolate, His Passion, His Resurrection, the Eucharist!

Who can measure, or try to understand, love such as this?

There is only one answer: to take up my cross and follow Him, slowly giving up all I possess.

Beloved, I love You and ask only to love You more and more! (April 4, 1935)

Keep a Guard over Your Heart

"Before all things, keep a guard over Your heart. For, from it, springs forth life." (*Prv 4:23*)

"This guard over my heart is nothing other than a watchful care, habitual or at least frequent, to preserve all my actions from anything that could corrupt my motives or their execution."[12]

Beloved, how far removed from all this I am! But I do want to develop my interior life because only in it is the source of the real apostolic activity.

O Beloved, I realize that a heart attached to the world or anything in it can't do it! Let me see myself clearly in that respect, for I think this is where I will have to work very hard. I am detached a little from material things; but my will, my human affections, my desire for human respect? O Beloved, please help me, You are the source of this inspiration. You have prompted in my heart the desire for all these things, the burning love for You.

O Beloved, leave me not, for by myself I can do nothing.
(April 5, 1935)

A Little Ring of Emptiness

"If God calls me to devote my energy not only to my personal sanctification, but also to good works, I shall establish this firm conviction before all else in my mind: Our Lord must be, and wishes to be, the life of these good works."[13]

Beloved, once more I thank You for this book. It is as if all the things I could not understand yet felt in my heart have been opened to my eyes. It is as if I was blind and now I see.

O dear Jesus, teach me and enlighten me. Give me the light of the Holy Spirit to see the steps to this interior life which is, above all, my goal. For years I have prayed to love You, love You, love You, and now You have shown me the way to this love. O Beloved, be blessed forever.

Slowly, in my mind the word "detachment" is taking shape. Detachment must be greater than what I understood it to be. It is an emptying of oneself in preparation for being filled by You. It is also a detachment from creatures as if one made a little ring of emptiness around oneself. It is also indifference to all things: praise and humiliation, heat or cold. Here, Jesus, I will stop, for this is what I must cultivate, isn't it? Indifference! Beloved, teach me. (April 6, 1935)

Jesus, Let Me See!

Jesus, Beloved, let me see! I am blind to my faults, blind to my sins, blind to the fact that I antagonize all people except those who themselves are saints and put up with me as a cross! I love You. Alone I can do nothing. Let me strive under Your guidance to get rid of my imperfections, no matter the cost. I am lonely because I deserve it. O Jesus, when I catch a glimpse of myself, I weep in horror at the picture. Help me, Beloved, to realize that You are all, I, nothing! Then will my pride be broken and in humility I will begin. Break my pride. Break it, O Jesus, even if it kills me. For with it I cannot have You and I want You above all. (April 7, 1935)

Inner Presence

"The life of action ought to flow from the contemplative life—interpret it, continue it outwardly, while being as little detached from it as possible."[14]

How right this is! The heart of the active person is like a well. God's grace is like the rain always falling from heaven and filling up the well for others to draw from. But there is much for an active person to do. Before he can begin any really worthwhile apostolate, how spotless must that heart be! How he must strive to be ready to cooperate with God's grace!

Beloved, will I ever understand this fully? When and if I understand, will I do it? For as I look at myself day by day, I could weep; I do weep. For I do not advance one iota. How shall I ever untangle the underbrush that grows in my soul?!

Beloved, look at it: briars of pride, thorns of self-will, bushes of vain-glory. O Jesus! O Mary! O Joseph! How will I begin, and where? Beloved, I want to. Slowly I want to clean myself of all these, and I want to make a garden of my soul for Your delight. Help me, Jesus. Help me, Beloved, for heavy is my heart and full of evil!

I see You and long for You, Beloved. Deep in my heart, I feel You and know my days are Yours. They pass through my hands like a rosary and drop at Your feet. But when, for a while, You are not the definite object of my efforts, I feel lost and unhappy and restless. Abide with me forever, Beloved. Do not leave me. Alone I cannot stand for a second. I love You.

(April 10, 1935)

Your Bridge of Love

"Remember Your word to Your servant, O Lord, by which You have given me hope!" (*Ps 119:49*)

It is only when I read the gospel that I realize Your tender beauty. It is a portrait of You. No, it is more. It is You. I stand entranced at Your love of us.

How can it be, indeed, for a God of majesty to come down and become human and then die for love? When I contemplate the Incarnation, the Eucharist, I know that only God could have conceived such a religion—only God!

O Beloved, let me fall prostrate and adore You. I love You. I love You. I love You. Teach me to love You more and more. Teach me to live with You, to reject anything that is not You, O Jesus. Help me, Beloved. Help me because without Your help I am nothing.

Daily I realize more the distance between You and Your creatures. Daily, I also see better the bridge of love You have established with them. O Beloved, teach me how to really love You! (April 11, 1935)

The Easiest Way to You

"All you who pass by the way, attend and see if there be any sorrow like to my sorrow." (*Lam 1:12*)

Your tender Mother has shared life and death with You. Is it to be wondered that at her feet we put all our sorrows, all our petitions, all our demands? She is one of us, yet how far above us! She understands the little things of men and women, our little preoccupations, our little thoughts and hopes and fears. But, also, she is the great Mediatrix between You and the world!

O Beloved, teach me to love Your mother—not with the cold, distant, respectful love of a slave to a mistress, or a poor person to his patron, or a man to his superior—No! Teach me to love with the warm, spontaneous love of a child for its mother. It is through her that we desire to offer You our small gifts of atonement: prayer, mortification and work—in a word, our life.

O Jesus, I know the shortest and easiest way to You is through Your Mother. Never allow my heart to become cold toward her. (April 12, 1935)

God Became Flesh

Factus is the word written on the tabernacle door of our parish church. *Et homo factus est*—and He became Man.

Factus...one word, Beloved. But what a wealth of joy and happiness, of sublime love, of perfect bliss. Factus. My God is here, factus. The Second Person of the Most Holy Trinity, factus.

Beloved, when I think of You, my heart just beats faster and faster. O Jesus, I love You. But do I love You enough; do I really realize what the word factus implies? Factus: that God became Incarnate, that Nazareth is true; that the hidden years are true; that the public ministry is true; that the Passion is true; that the Crucifixion is true; that the Resurrection is true; that Transubstantiation, the daily miracle, is true; that the Real Presence is true!

Factus. I see the word as I receive Holy Communion. Factus, I tremble with fear. For, if love has done that, then what is justice going to be like? O Beloved, where are Your children? The churches are empty in the daytime. They are filled on Sundays, but so many are absent who should be there. And yet, daily, the miracle of love takes place; daily, bread and wine become God!

Beloved, I adore You. Prostrate, I lie in the dust before You who have become Man. I believe You are Christ, come down to save sinners. Adoring You, I ask for love, a love that knows no limit, a love like a flame that consumes me. O Christ, O Lord, one gift I ask of You: love for You everincreasing, ever-growing, ever-active on Your behalf!   (April 14, 1935)

Direct Me, Jesus

Direct me, my Jesus, into the right way because I do not seem able to change. O Beloved, every day I start, only to find out by the end of the day, I have fallen again. I have been an utter failure, Beloved. How You can stand the sight of me is beyond my grasp. O darling Lord, have mercy on me, a sinner. I seem to have lost my head just as a child has lost its mother's hand. Beloved, do not leave me; I am Your very own.

(April 14, 1935)

Passion Week

Beloved, once more, on my knees, I face another day. My heart is heavy, for it is Monday of Holy Week, the week of Your crucifixion. As I follow Your Passion with You, my heart seems to break and tears come to my eyes. Jesus, Son of God, come down to save us sinners, and have mercy on me, the greatest sinner of them all.

This week, my life, in comparison to Your Passion, leaves me aghast! True, I weep. But I ask You more: grant to me, this Holy Week, the light to better understand the enormity of sin, the infinity of Your love, the greatness of Your mercy, and having understood better, to run to do my work. Let Your word, "I am thirsty,"[15] echo and re-echo in my soul, never allowing me any rest. Souls! You want souls! Let me—by practicing the works of mercy, by loving You, by living in You—let me, I beg You, bring souls to You. Alone, I know I cannot do anything. But with You and through You, I can.

O Beloved, let Your slightest wish be my command. Let Your will ever be my only desire.

O Jesus, Beloved, I want to be with You through the Passion at Gethsemane, everywhere. But, above all, I want to be at the foot of the Cross. May I? Like Magdalene? I have sinned much. You have forgiven much. My place is with You in reparation. O Beloved, I love, love, love You. Give me light to love You more and more. (April 15, 1935)

You and the Cross

"It behooves us to glory in the cross of Jesus Christ."[16]

Beloved, Your cross! Whenever one thinks at all of You, one must also think of the cross. You and the cross are inseparable. You have glorified it by Your death, spoken of it all Your life, and made it a necessity for Your followers. "Take up your cross and follow me."[17] And the Holy Eucharist is Calvary, and Calvary is the cross and God on it!

Beloved, why is the world so afraid of the cross? Why is it so unwise as not to see that it is only through the cross they will find You? They have forgotten You and the cross.

Yesterday, as I went to church, I saw the world moving toward pleasure. Beloved, I do not want the world. I want You and the cross. For I know Your burden is light! I have glimpsed its secret delights. I have understood that, losing all, I gain all! O Jesus, help, help me, help me to serve You better.

What do I desire to obtain? Lord, I want to open my heart before You, to lay bare my miseries and place my hopes at Your feet! I desire holy recollection, spiritual silence, detachment and poverty of spirit. I want to fight the world, the devil, the flesh.

Any moment You want me, My Lord, I will get up and follow You. (April 18, 1935)

There Is Nothing I Can Refuse You

Dear Lord, as I behold You dying on the cross, I feel there is nothing I can refuse You. I see that You must be a jealous lover, for You have given us so much, so terribly much—all of Yourself—even to Your terrible death on the cross. How can I love anyone else but You?   (April 19, 1935)

The Graces of Lent

Beloved, today I want to thank You for the great graces of Lent. This Lent has been so precious to me, so wonderful. Hidden truths have become clear, and my own heart's desire definite: You.

O Beloved, thank You for Your kindness, Your mercy, Your forgiveness, Your love. I ask of You only one gift for myself on this glorious Easter: to love You ever more! I offer You the poorest gift anyone ever gave: my heart, all of myself.

You asked for it: "I am thirsty."[18] It is Yours to do with as You wish. Only, with the penitent thief, I repeat, "Lord, remember me when You come into Your Kingdom."[19]

I love, love, love You. And I rejoice today at the approaching beauty of Your Resurrection!   (April 20, 1935)

Christ Is Risen!

Alleluia! Alleluia! Alleluia! This is the day! Rejoice and be glad! Christ is risen! Beloved, I love You! I adore You! I thank You! Because of Your death, we have life. Because of Your resurrection, we have faith.

O Jesus, beloved Friend, Master, I believe, I love, I thank, I adore! Teach me to always keep Your peace; to always walk before Your face; to always remember Your commandment, "Love one another as I have loved you."[20]

Beloved, the day is fair. My heart overflows with love and gratitude. I have only my heart to offer. Here it is! You fashioned it; You made it! It is Yours as I am Yours: memory, will, intellect, body, soul, heart, all my faculties. Beloved, keep me in Your heart, for I was made for You!   (April 21, 1935)

The Road to Emmaus

"They knew Him in the breaking of the bread." (*Jn 24:35*)

Beloved, as I read the gospel of today it seems my flesh can't stand it. I feel hot and cold and frightened with the glorious meaning of it all! Your thoughtfulness in hiding Yourself from Your disciples, I understand that, for unless sustained by Your grace, I think I would die if I ever were to see You before my appointed time.

Jesus, my Lord, I worship You. I love You. I desire to love You more and more. I believe. (April 22, 1935)

To Always Speak of You

"Declare His deeds among the nations!" (*Ps 95:3*)

Beloved, this is my dream: to always speak of You. I get so tired of talking or hearing about little uninteresting things, gossip and so forth, when our lifetime is too short to talk about Your beauty, Your majesty, Your love, Your condescension.

O Jesus, my heart is aflame with love for You; my tongue never, never will cease to praise You. My daily work, because of Your generosity, is to talk about You, Beloved, to work for You. Bless it, because its whole root is You. I am nothing. The work is nothing. You are everything: its source, its *raison d'être*, its end.

Beloved, often I think of the work of the Church, my humble effort included, as the radiation of Your Sacred Heart, a sun of love. Its rays strike our hearts and reflect from ours into others and so on, ad infinitum. As they travel, the rays beget warmth and light. They are the spiritual and corporal works of mercy. The strength and length of the rays depend on the condition of our hearts; without Your generating love, they die. O Jesus, I love You. May I do all things in You!

(April 23, 1935)

The Interior Life

"The interior life is the state of activity of a soul which strives against its natural inclinations, in order to regulate them, and endeavors to acquire the habit of judging and acting in everything according to the light of the gospel and the examples of our Lord."[21]

This is the goal of my life. The feeling has been in my heart so long. I know the road is not easy. I know it means absolute severance from the world and all it stands for. But what of it? I know I have the better part. Poverty spells freedom. Work for God spells freedom. Work for God spells happiness. Obedience spells self-mastery. Charity, the hardest of all, spells nearness to God, the source of life.

I know I am right. Therefore, with Your grace, Beloved, I will strive toward this goal, interior life through Your example. Help me, for the reason for my desire is pure love. I love You! True, I am frail, sinful and weak, but it is for such as me that You have come. As I reflect on Your words at various times, I see You as the Good Physician, the Shepherd, the Savior of sinners. Give me the grace to realize that You died and were incarnated for each of us. That also means me! If my Lord and my God did this out of love for me, what is there for me to do, but give my life to Him. Here I am, O Lord, broken up, sinful, weak, miserable, yet Your slave. I may diverge from the path, but I will never leave it, for my heart is in Your heart and my soul has loved You forever.   (April 30, 1935)

Contemplation

"To devote oneself to the life of prayer or to contemplation pleases the Lord more than to give oneself to good works."[22]

Beloved, make me realize this and give me the grace to make others realize it with me because it is the foundation of life. Give me, O Lord, the light to see the way, the strength to follow it when I see it, and the love to stay on it when other ways open themselves before me!

Today, prostrate at Your feet, I pray for all those who labor that they may see the light of the Carpenter and go the right way.   (May 1, 1935)

Channels

"Men and women called to the honor of working with the Savior must look upon themselves as simple channels whose work is to draw from this unique source."[23]

Beloved, let this simple principle sink deeply into my heart. Let me never, never allow myself even a glow of satisfaction in myself for I am nothing. Help me to rejoice in Your glory in as much as my apostolate is successful, for it is so through Your grace. It is Your grace which draws me to this work. It is Your grace which makes it possible for me to continue in it. It is Your grace again that gives me strength. It is Your grace that uses me, unfit as I am, as an instrument. It is Your grace that draws men and women through me to Yourself. I am but the channel, and Your grace even cleans and fashions the channel.

O Jesus, help me to see clearly and, seeing clearly, to recognize the first principle of active work—union with You. All things in You, and in You only, Beloved. Help me to see and to make others see. I pledge myself again and again, daily, only to work for love of You and for Your glory. Help me to keep this pledge. Increase my love for You, Beloved, for in it alone will I find strength, O Jesus.

Help me, Mary, once more. I do want to be faithful to Your Son! Help me, Mother of all graces!   (May 3, 1935)

Christ in Me

"And I live, not I, but Christ in me." (*Gal 2:20*)

Beloved, to achieve this I must erect no obstacles. I must think, judge, love, will, suffer, work with You, by You, in You. All my exterior actions must reflect Your life in my soul! To do this, I must prepare my soul for You, Beloved; it must be in a state of grace. But that is not enough. I must adorn it with meekness, humility, detachment, poverty of spirit, mortification, unselfishness, charity. I, dust, am nothing. I, unfit to lie on the ground where You have stood, must prepare myself as a fit abode for my God.

Can this be done? Only with Your grace! So, on my knees, I beg for it. To Your Mother, I run and beseech her to grant me this grace, Your grace, to love You so as to at least try with all my soul, with all my heart, to prepare my soul for You.

O, Jesus, how I love You; I want to love You more and more.   (May 4, 1935)

Temptation

"Out of the depths I have cried to You, O Lord. Lord hear my voice." (*Ps 130:1*)

Beloved, hear my voice for I am in the depth of temptation. From all sides I am besieged by them because they rage within me. O Beloved, I have fought the good fight. I have tried to do as You say, to keep Your commandments and, above all, I love You so. I cannot live without You for a moment. Mortal sin horrifies me for it separates me from You.

Beloved, on my knees I pray, not for the removal of temptation, but for the strength to fight it. Keep me clean and spotless in Your heart.   (May 5, 1935)

A Gray Day

My Lord, today is a gray day in my soul with distaste for everything spiritual, a desire to run away from it, forget it, to live in the world of senses with music, human joys. Every word of prayer is an effort; I find every excuse for not going to Mass, feel every desire to shirk. Inside, I feel a dryness that simply kills every thought. Meditation is hard; no, impossible. There are distractions in all things I do. I have a sense of overpowering loneliness. I have nothing left but God—His grace and my free will—but God seems so far away as to be non-existent.

His grace? I do not feel it. All is dark on the spiritual side. Yet I know I love Him. I know He is there. I believe, Lord; help my unbelief.

I ask for only one thing today: the will to hold on—to go to church when I seem to find every step leaden; to pray when all the distractions in the world assail me. At least give me the grace to say the words for today I seem unable to do more. Give me the will to hold on in spite of everything. I do not feel it but I repeat and shall repeat all day: I love You, Lord. Have mercy on me a sinner. All is a burden. All is night. My faith is dimmed. I will hold on. Help me. I feel lost, weak, unstable.

O Beloved, give me strength! (May 6, 1935)

Amen

Beloved: Amen. Just a little word but what a profound significance to it. Today I say amen to all the bruises and pain in my heart. Amen to the misery of my soul in the last two days. Amen to all pain from everywhere and to all of God's will for everyone. Amen even to the bewildering maze of new pain and tragedy.

I feel beaten up morally, mentally, physically. In You alone is my hope, Beloved. I hang onto the cross only with the power of faith. For all my other faculties are numb. But I know the cross is my refuge—just to hold on at all cost! (May 12, 1935)

A Furnace of Doubts

Lord, my soul is a furnace of temptations, doubts and difficulties again. Daily I see Your precepts flouted, not only by the rich, but by priests, Your chosen ones. The misery of the world cries out, only to meet cowardly silence. The Pope speaks; no one listens. The majority live in ease and affluence which shines oddly against the background of poverty. The followers of the Nazarene? Corruption, bribes, selfishness, greed reign supreme! Relentlessly, Communism beats like high waves at the shore of the world! Where to go? Where to turn? One spot is sure—Christ and His Church—if only it were not filled with Judases and Pilates at their worst!

O Lord, help me. Bewildered, hurt, bleeding for the masses, suffering, miserable, lonely, I am racked with pain, O Jesus! Lord and Master, I submit, but I cannot understand. Help me. Help me in this darkness of mind, soul and body.

(May 18, 1935)

The Meaning of Words

Beloved, how hard it is for us mortals to fully realize the meaning of words. "Mortal sins," for instance, is just two words. Yet they imply such a tremendous, almost unthinkable thought of expelling God from our souls where He dwells as the Most Holy Trinity! It means the rejection of the Fatherhood of God, the Brotherhood of Christ! It means shutting the Holy Spirit out of our souls! It means allowing Satan in through his operatives: malice, hate, envy. All this though "mortal sin" is just two words. (May 21, 1935)

Humility

Humility: here lies the secret of sanctity. Pride is the most subtle, the most plausible vice of all. It sets up such a lot of absolutely logical statements. It was pride, for instance, which urged me to resign from my work, with the idea that I was hindering it. It was pride which called on me to give up because I was unworthy. It is perfectly obvious that I am unworthy, and that I am nothing, but it is God's delight to use bad instruments—nullities—to show off His glory. It is not for me to question, but to cooperate. Yet pride steps in, and wrecks the whole edifice.

O Jesus, help me to cultivate the very spirit of humility: not to seek pleasure, comfort, gratification from others; not to worry about what the outcome will be for me; to bear all the humiliations and persecutions, Jesus, for love of You. It is Your work. O Jesus, I love You. Teach me to learn from You for You are meek and humble of heart. (May 25, 1935)

Teach Me Your Ways

O Jesus, teach me Your ways; make me realize profoundly, fully, the richness of a life hidden in You. Without You, there is nothing. Without You there is no life, just death. Help me to understand that only through You and by You, are all things. Let my life be dedicated to You through Your poor and needy. Never allow me to lose sight of You, for even in the smallest things I can work only through You. Allow me the privilege of bringing men and women to You. Make me a fit instrument of Your glory. Influence my heart with an all-consuming love of You. (May 26, 1935)

Ask and You Shall Receive
"Ask and you shall receive, that your joy may be full." (*Mt* 7:7)

Beloved, only You, our God, could have said such a thing as that, graciously generous and joyful to the extreme! And we, fools that we are, do not believe You! We try to gather into our small hands gold and silver, stones and papers, and we think we are wealthy.

Fools! Fools! Paupers! That is what we are, for we do not possess You and do not know the wealth of poverty, the kingdom of meekness, the gold of service, the myrrh of suffering.

I am not beyond the desires of ordinary people, but I possess God! He dwells in me in His Trinity; He comes to me in the Eucharist! How can I be tempted by tinsel? Ask for the heart of life and you will possess all things. (May 27, 1935)

Jesus, Be at Home in My Heart
O my Lord, I love You beyond anyone or anything I have ever loved or can love. I adore You. I know You dwell in my soul. And yet, I allow it to be filled with so many things besides You. I am loath to clean house because my detachment is not complete. I am still attached to my own will, to certain people, to certain comforts. Teach me to get rid of them. Teach me to recognize them. Teach me to overcome myself and them.

I realize how near You are. Your mercy shines like a light, and my sins are as if they were not. How wonderful it is to be so close to You. The birds, the flowers, the grass, the stars and heaven all speak of You. The rest of the world is far away. As I behold it now, I can see in it love of creatures, self-will, love of comfort, vainglory. Help me to be rid of them.

(June 9, 1935)

I Marvel at Your Love

"O the depths of the riches of wisdom and of the knowledge of God." (*Rom 11:33*)

Today, my heart stands in love and awe before these great words of St. Paul. The thought comes to me not to wonder that I love You, but to marvel that You love me. As the mystery of Your love unfolds before me in the Incarnation, the Redemption, I realize more and more my utter nothingness. What am I? Just clay, dust. Yet, through Your love, I am God-like. I am a God-bearer.

O Jesus, Lord and Master, I fall at Your feet and adore You with all the love and the power of my soul. I am Yours to do with as You please. Teach me to see Your will in all events. Teach me as You have taught the bee to gather honey from flowers. Teach me to gather Your pleasure in all things that befall me. Make me realize that, far from being a source of misery, humiliation, persecution, gossip, revilement and misunderstandings are but opportunities to share Your Passion, avenues of sacrifice and merit.

I have made my choice. I want to be wherever You are. I want to follow You to the end. Yes, I know Your end was Calvary; Your way was the Way of the Cross. It will also be mine.

I know that, alone, I cannot make it, for all comes from You, all goes through You, and all leads to Your glory. So humbly and simply I ask, "Take my hands and lead me." It is You who have put the desire to follow You into my heart. It is to You that I turn when the cross You have chosen for me seems too heavy. It is to You I look when, bruised and bleeding, I cannot walk any more.

Here I am, O Most Holy Trinity—in my nothingness and unworthiness, Your fool, Your child—Yours to do with as You please. I need Your help; alone I cannot do anything. I love You. I adore You. (June 16, 1935)

I Stand in Awe

O Beloved, how good You are to me, how consoling in Your friendship and kindness. Forever I find You at the corner that seems a blank wall. Always You are near me when I do not know where to turn! When I fall, You are there telling me to rise; when I am sorrowful, You console me. O Jesus, I love You; teach me to love You more and more.

When I look back I stand in awe before Your incredible ways! You have taken me, a sinful creature of no account whatsoever, and You have used me as an instrument of Your will. Beloved, Beloved, blessed be Your will.

Here I stand naked before You with only these things to offer You: my love for You and my desire to serve You, both given to me by Your grace. I am, of all creatures, the most unworthy, as You well know. And since I am so far down, give me, O You who delight in showering creatures with Your gifts, give me the grace to love You more and more!

(June 22, 1935)

Lord, Let Your Will Be Mine

Beloved, the more I think and meditate on abandonment, the clearer my thought becomes: it is immaterial what weapon I use in my spiritual life, what ways I follow, as long as I do Your will. I find it expressed in people, things, and events, and by rules of life, and desires of superiors. Prayer, contemplation, and other activities—good as they are in themselves—are good for me only if You will them for me.

Beloved, help me to practice what, in His grace, the Holy Spirit has made understandable to me.   (June 25, 1935)

The Duty of the Present Moment

"A soul cannot be truly nourished, strengthened, purified, enriched, sanctified except by the fullness of the present moment."[24]

O Beloved, teach me the wisdom of these words. Teach me to accept suffering, irritations, pain, especially heart pain, as trials allowed by You for my sanctification. Teach me quietness and joyful reception of all. Teach me that, at all moments, Your will is the best.

Every hour I am amazed by Your love toward me, astonished at Your kindness and condescension. What You did for me—that You are present in the Blessed Sacrament for me—is a bewildering mystery just as is the fact that You have chosen me, so sinful, so vile, so utterly no-good to be an instrument of Your work. I do not understand. I simply accept and abandon myself into Your hands as a child unto the bosom of her mother. (June 26, 1935)

Thank You for the Great Joy

Beloved, thank You for the great joy of today's Communion. How brilliant the light of faith was! How profoundly did I realize what St. Peter was saying, "You are the Christ, the Son of the Living God!"[25] Just for a second, I knew it to be so. Now my whole soul and heart are lifted in love and faith and in adoration.

A moment? Yes, indeed, only a moment, but a moment for life. O Beloved, I cannot fathom why You are so good to me, but I adore and love and thank You for it. (June 29, 1935)

To Be a Saint

Teach me to love and obey Your holy will. I do not desire anything else. Teach me to recognize it in daily life, in the little things of which it is composed.

Help me to become a saint. Saints are great lovers of God and of men and women, and that is what I want to be. Beloved, I love You, but I always want to love You more and more, and through You and for You, to love people more and more too.

Daily, I see so much misery based on Your absence, or perhaps on lack of recognition of Your presence. Beloved, help me to lead them to You. (June 29, 1935)

You Know My Loves

"Detach yourself from creatures and completely abandon yourself to the will of God."[26]

Beloved here he raises the first real difficulty in my spiritual life. You know my real self; You know my loves; You know my life. You know how affectionate I really am, how profoundly I become attached to some people. But one thing I can truthfully say with all my heart, is that I would at any time gladly leave in your hands the care of all those I love, even my son. I love them in You, as much as I understand how! (July 2, 1935)

Your Presence

"There is no moment when God is not present with us under the appearance of some obligation or some duty."[27]

Beloved, teach me to realize that You are present in all things. Teach me to see in all interruptions, in all difficulties, in all trials, only Your hands leading me to perfection. Teach me to pierce the disguise of events and see Your face and understand Your will. Teach me, Beloved. Teach me to quietly let myself go on the sea of Your will. You know all. You see all. Into Your hands I place all. (July 4, 1935)

Return to You

Beloved, it is as if a new life has come into my veins. I feel happy, contented, and lifted up. Once more my inner life is regulated by You. How desolate a week without Masses! How desolate and lonely. How little we realize what You mean to us until You are taken away. O Beloved, help me.

(July 17, 1935)

It Is So Hard to Submit

Beloved, it is so hard to submit every moment to Your will. I want to, and yet daily, hourly, minute by minute, I am in rebellion against it. O Jesus, help me to overcome myself, my desire to dominate, to rule. Remind me it is so much better to serve than to command. Change my heart inside. Why do I have to be always irritated? Why? Help me. O Jesus, I am a sinner!

(July 18, 1935)

Teach Me to Pray Always

Teach me to pray, Jesus. Not long flowery orations, but a continual prayer, a perpetual offering of all my moments.

Sweet Lord, prayer should be like breathing, each moment uniting the soul of the creature with that of the Creator. O Jesus, what an immense grace, what perfect happiness! Jesus, teach me to pray.

(July 21, 1935)

Inner Listening

"God speaks; it is a mystery."[28]

Beloved, my soul seems happy listening. I think it must be for Your footsteps or perhaps for the Holy Spirit. He comes quietly, as a soft evening wind. And after His passing, my soul is joyous, refreshed.

(July 23, 1935)

Suffering and Action

"We only know perfectly that which we have learned by experience through suffering and action."[29]

O Beloved, is this why You train me so thoroughly in wide experience of constant action and continual suffering? Blessed be Your name. Each day brings rebuffs and sorrow and humiliations; each day trials and profound suffering.

O Beloved, I rejoice because You allow me to take part in Your life. Nobody but You knows the tragedies of which my life is full. I just have to carry on, O Jesus. How little people understand it, Beloved. Indeed Your yoke is sweet and light. My heart is full of peace and light and Your glory. O Jesus, I love You.

Someday, I'll have to walk up to Calvary and be crucified with You. Amen, I am ready because I love You.

(July 26, 1935)

The Duty of the Moment is the Duty of God

"The present moment is like an ambassador which declares the will of God."[30]

Beloved, here lies a little secret: "The duty of the moment is the duty of God." How few of us realize it. This is one thing in which I want to train myself: to listen only to Your will and pick up or drop, do or stop, pray or work at Your will. It is hard for me because I have no superior, only the Spirit and circumstances to tell me Your will. O Jesus, help me. I love You. (July 28, 1935)

Poverty

"The secret of union with God is within the reach of all. Avail yourself of all He sends you. All things may further this union; all things perfect it, save sin, and that which is contrary to your duty. You have but to accept all He sends and let it do its work in you."[31]

Beloved, how simple and how difficult to understand! Give me light to see it all and grace to act when I see. My whole soul craves to devote my life to You, to immerse myself in You, to live and die for You. But events do not seem to allow me this wish. Ties of blood, works of mercy, keep me chained. I crave poverty as others crave riches. I desire to imitate You, to be poor for Your sake, but You do not seem to allow me this wish. May Your will be done in all things, O Beloved. Teach me to be poor and detached in spirit. Jesus, I love You.

(July 31, 1935)

I Will Be Your Disciple

"My dear love! I will be Your disciple. I will learn in no other school but Yours."[32]

Beloved, days merge into weeks, weeks into years, and still I am not advancing in my particular virtues! Beloved, only You would put up with me in Your inexhaustible patience. I love You, Jesus. I want to serve You. Yet I am such an absolutely unworthy pupil—dull, dense, attracted by silvery glitter, by every noise. I do not carry out the lessons learned at Your feet. I seem to stride in long strides and get nowhere.

O Jesus, have pity on me. Help me to learn. Help me to put my learning into practice. No more arguments. Silence and peace—these I will try to put into my life day by day. I have to start at the bottom. Teach me, O Holy Spirit.

(August 1, 1935)

Life's Miseries

"Receive into the depth of Your being the waters of that sea of bitterness which inundated the soul of Christ."[33]

Dear Lord, as I journey through life, more and more I see the truth that sorrow, misery, tears and difficulties attend every day of our lives. We can moan under them and be crushed, or we can accept them, uniting ourselves to Your sorrow, O Jesus.

Slowly the light of abandonment to Your will begins to dawn on me—another grace from You, Beloved. Teach me to be happy in all life's events because all of them are presented by You for my sanctification. Beloved, I love You. Forgive my sins and teach me to do Your will in every little thing.

(August 6, 1935)

Rely on God

"The more He deprives us of natural aid, the more He gives us of the supernatural."[34]

Beloved, as I look upon my life, especially in the last years, I see clearly how, one by one, all human aids, props and so forth are being taken away from me, and how I am seemingly left in mid-air. How alone and lost I feel. Even the best seem to turn against me, O Jesus. On the other side, my attraction for You grows. How many hundreds of little threads draw me toward You! Daily, You fill part and then all of my horizon. I love You. And You, in Your mercy, increase my love.

At times, as I look upon myself, I do not recognize myself. How changed I am! What was of interest yesterday is gone today.

Beloved, help me to see, and seeing, to understand and run to You leaving all human aids aside. Help me to stay at Your feet—pliant, submissive, loving and obedient to Your will.

(August 7, 1935)

The Divine Will of God

"All the events of the world can only work the good of souls perfectly submissive to the divine will of God."[35]

O Beloved, teach me to see this truth. Teach me to act on it when I see it. I love You so. I want so much to be close to You, pliant and good, humble and chaste, abandoned to Your Holy will.

Again a day has passed in which I have not prayed or deliberately lifted my heart to You. Yet I have a feeling of Your presence. It is more subconscious than conscious. I feel You are in me and I in You. When things that hurt me happen during the day, I instinctively hide myself in Your Heart.

Still, Jesus, I am sorry You are not on my lips as much as You should be.   (August 8, 1935)

It Is God Who Saves

"The Divine Action justifies her. Since the work is God's, from no other source must its justification be sought."[36]

Beloved, how I wish this would penetrate my heart—not to justify myself, not to explain or excuse. O Jesus, when? When will I at last start on the ladder of perfection? I have so wanted to for years and yet I have not done so! Will it be never? I love You so and yet I am as a piece of wood, not even shaped. As for all Your great graces, I have tried so hard to cooperate with them, Beloved! Yet I never do. O Jesus, teach me to be obedient to the last degree.   (August 9, 1935)

Aches and Pains

"Thus, souls abandoned to God's will take no heed of their infirmities."[37]

Beloved, how right this is. How I pamper my body! How I worry about it and my infirmities! Yet what do they matter when I can put them to a glorious use? Jesus, I love You. I want to start to repeat this every day because the reason for my work, my life, is You. I want to work for You, by You, through You. Jesus, I love You.   (August 10, 1935)

The Road to Sainthood

I have done so little on this road, but trusting You completely and fully, and realizing Your boundless mercy, I throw myself upon it and ask the grace to start once more. I will not burden myself with many unnecessary practices. I will simply pray to have a little secret with You. I want to start to be faithful to You in little aspirations, in lifting my heart to You. I choose two: "Jesus, I love You," and "Jesus, I trust You absolutely." Please darling Lord, help me to do this little thing faithfully and daily.

Lately I have been very happy. All goes wrong in one way; yet all goes well in another. There is so much I have to hope for only from You. Yet I have seldom been so at peace and so full of trust in You.

Beloved, help me. I love You!   (August 11, 1935)

A Hidden Saint

O Jesus, help me to become a saint—not a known one—no. Make me a little hidden one known only to You. Beloved, slowly I want to start on little things that others will not notice. I want our little secret to grow. It is making me happy that little secret. The short prayers are coming back spontaneously and already I see the results. They quiet irritation. Help me to gather a very tiny bouquet of bodily mortifications for You as well. I will try to reduce bread and butter and sugar in my diet. It is the hardest for me to do but I will try it. Help me, especially to train myself in it until my will hardens.

Help me, Jesus, to be a hidden saint. The magnitude of the task is huge, but all is possible, to You.   (August 13, 1935)

Make Me Generous

"We must not be cowardly, but generous as becomes souls chosen to do God's work."[38]

Good morning, Beloved! As a child runs to its parents to be petted and kissed, I run to You. I offer You all I have: my will, my understanding, my memory, myself—all that I am—for indeed, You are the author of it all.

I ask only:

1) Your blessing on me and my work
2) Faith, absolute faith unto abandonment
3) Love of chastity, poverty, obedience
4) Love of You increasing daily
5) Souls, souls, souls.

Is this too much? Or is it too little? I do not know. I ask simply, remembering what You said: "Ask and you shall receive."[39]

O Beloved, thank You for all You have done for me. I adore You and love You as my sovereign. O Jesus! O Jesus!

(August 15, 1935)

To Hide in Your Heart

O Beloved, Your learned teachers speak well from books, but somehow, I love to run to You, hide myself in Your Sacred Heart, give myself to You and then remain very still inside or go about Your work. Deep, deep in my soul I like always to listen to You, Your voice, Your desires. I like to talk to You or be very still at Your feet. Silence is so eloquent at times. Jesus, I love You so very much. Teach me to love You more!

(August 17, 1935)

Fight

Beloved, it is indeed clear to me that what You desire of me is to fight myself, because my first duty is to save myself—my immortal soul—and that means a continual fight. Please teach me to go about it in the right way, to listen carefully to my conscience, to understand it is Your voice quietly speaking to me. I am Yours, Jesus, with all my will, but my senses are strong. They fight my will. Help me. I want to be Yours because I love You.   (August 20, 1935)

The Blessed Sacrament

Beloved, will You forgive me for my neglect of You in the Blessed Sacrament? Will You forgive me for coming only in the morning and not visiting You in the daytime? Will You teach my wayward heart to pray before You in the Blessed Sacrament all the time!

Beloved, teach me to work and go about Your business with a heart lost in adoration of You, kneeling in my mind at the foot of the altar all day. It should be easy, but see how my mind returns to its earthly loves one thousand times a day? Are You not many times more precious, Beloved? Draw my heart into Your Sacred Heart until I am lost in it. I love You. I trust You. I am all Yours, Beloved.   (August 23, 1935)

A Thief in the Night

Beloved, what is it that comes like a thief in the night? Temptations of the flesh—vivid, beautiful, strong and enticing—they surround one with passion. The world looks rosy. Mind and will cease to function. The body glows supreme!

O Beloved, how far away You seem. I feel lost, alone in a darkness of warmth, sounds and images, alone with desires like fire with pictures of love and light and laughter. Prayer, work, Mass, Communion—all are distasteful and hard. O Jesus, have pity on Your child. I am so lonely, so hungry for love and companionship. Have mercy on me. Help me. Help me.

(August 26, 1935)

Love of the Poor

Beloved, I have heard the whisper of Your voice, seen the imprint of Your feet, risen and followed You. I love You, love You, love! Give me this broad understanding of love for Your poor, this fire that burns Your heart and gives of itself. O Beloved, I am seeking You day and night. I know where to find You: in myself and in Your poor.   (August 27, 1935)

Your Beauty

Beloved, I love You so! At times I get little glimpses of Your love for me, but I am afraid of stopping and thinking and feeling it out. It is so vast, so incredible, so lovely: God loves me! O Jesus, You are the one wonderful reality in this life, the one perfect thing.   (August 28, 1935)

A Blazing Faith

Beloved, Your gift to me is blazing faith, an enthusiastic service. Do not take it away from me, Beloved. It is the only thing I can give back to You unspotted. Beloved, I love You. I am Yours.   (August 29, 1935)

I Fall Again

"Be gone, Satan. For it is written, 'the Lord your God you shall adore and Him only shall you serve.'" (*Mt 4:10*)

Beloved, how is it that all my love for You, all my desire to express it in words and deeds, do not keep me completely away from sin? At least it should help me to overcome temptations. I profess to be Yours; I assure You of my love; I receive innumerable graces from You. I fall again.

O Beloved, have pity on me a sinner. I love You. I love You. I love! I do not want to sin. I beg fervently to have the occasion of sin removed, although I must be quiet, tranquil, accept temptations and fight them, praying for Your help and grace. O Beloved, if only I could conquer for a while all my vileness and sin and love You!

Forgive me, Jesus, but somehow I feel so lost, and at times so bewildered by evil in me, around me. I want to weep. You brought so much beauty to us. Why must humanity wallow in filth? (August 31, 1935)

From Childhood, I Have Loved You

"I will love You, O Lord, my strength." (*Ps 18:1*)

Beloved, from childhood I have loved You. All my life I have prayed to You to kindle a furnace of love for You in my heart. I want to love You to the exclusion of everything else.

O Jesus, light of my soul, inflame my heart with a fire of love for You, and then let me be the Good Samaritan always. Let me see my neighbor in all people. Let me serve them joyfully and with love.

Beloved, give me the knowledge of the secret of the saints who could always act against themselves because they loved You. I want to imitate St. Francis Xavier and do all things—the biggest and smallest—only out of love for You. I want to acquire the spirit of St. Francis of Assisi and give up all things for love of You. I want to be like St. Catherine of Siena and deal with the worst of humanity for love of You.

O Jesus, I love You. When I contemplate Your desire for our love, I am lost in a mystery past my understanding: You, God, pleading for the love of Your creatures! I do not understand, but I adore Your holy will, and prostrate before You, I implore the gift of loving You absolutely.

I am such a nothing, I cannot even love You without Your own grace to do so! Beloved, help me to tear out all things and creatures that do not help me to love You more.

(September 1, 1935)

You Are Beauty

"Make straight the way where I should walk, for I have lifted my soul unto You!" (*Ps 143:8*)

Beloved, indeed I have lifted my soul unto You. Slowly, You are granting my one prayer: to give me the grace to love

You with all my mind, my soul, my heart, my thoughts—with all of me to the exclusion of all other things. Give me the grace to love people and the world of creatures and creation only in You, through You and for You.

It is as if You are always present with me—at some times vividly, overwhelmingly; at other times dimly; at others in only a shallow way. Yet always I know if You are pleased or displeased. It is as if You are permeating my actions and my thoughts in a subconscious way which I find hard to understand and harder still to explain.

O Jesus, Beloved, how beautiful is Your service. Why is it that the world grasps at fleeting shadows and dim reflections of beauty, which are only reflections of You, when it can have You—the only reality in the world—Beauty complete!

Beloved, give me the gift of love so I can go out and serve You and love You and help You in my neighbors. This is my thought: to give all up for You. Slowly, I grasp the beauty of Holy Poverty! I dimly begin to see why St. Francis wooed her so passionately. It is a short cut to You. Jesus, help me to be poor in spirit and in fact. Teach me to love You, Lord. Dimly I see You are all beautiful. You are beauty.

(September 2, 1935)

Death
"The day of the Lord will come like a thief." (*2 Pt 3:10*)

Indeed, Beloved, I know not when You will come. But, daily, my desire for Your arrival grows. I used to be afraid of death. But now, since I have realized that it is just the last step to You, I welcome death. O Beloved, it is easy to face death knowing You will be there to meet me. But it is not easy for me to pray for death, as I want to put my whole life into Your hands. I ask only the grace of Viaticum, if such is Your will.

Now there is life. I want it to be all for You. I want it to be such that I would be ready for You at all times. Take me now, all of me, as Ignatius Loyola says, "my will, my memory, my understanding, all my faculties," for they, as all else, have been given to me by You, Beloved. What better use can I put them to than Your service?

Often, I want to shout and thank You and sing for sheer joy and happiness when I realize all You have given me: the grace to love You, the desire to serve You, membership in Your Church, all the blessings of Your Church, love of the poor, a child, friendships that light my life, and, daily, Yourself, O Jesus.

Thank You, thank You, Beloved.   (September 4, 1935)

What I Crave to Do

"The Lord will reward me according to my justice; and will repay me according to the cleanliness of my hands." (*Ps 18:20*)

Why is it, Jesus, so few—even my best friends—understand what I crave to do? You know! I know You know, for isn't it You who have put the desire for poverty into my heart? Jesus, how I long to be poor, to acquire the inner spirit of detachment and poverty, even though others do not understand that it will make me free.

Darling Jesus, help me to grow in poverty; help me to love it profoundly. Help me, when I must use the things of my station in life, not to enjoy them for themselves, not to become attached to them, but just to use them because I must! O Jesus, You know how I want to follow in Your footsteps. There are so many things in my heart; You put them there. Bring them out in my life.

Beloved, make me all Yours. I am nothing; I am unworthy. But I am precious because You died for me. You make my soul priceless. Help me to give it to You.   (September 5, 1935)

The Cross

"If anyone wishes to come after me... let him take his cross and follow me." (*Lk 9:23*)

Beloved, how many times I have read these words. Have they penetrated my heart, soul and mind? Have I taken up my cross of small annoyances, of difficulties, and sorrows each day?

Dear Jesus, when shall I realize the depth of this precept. I love You. I can reach You only through the cross. Why is it, then, that I hesitate? Why is it that I tremble at the approach of suffering? Make me brave, for love is as strong as death, and I love You. Give me the gift of love for You again and again. I beg it of You, a love so overwhelming that I would run and welcome suffering for reparation's sake, a love so great that I would become poor and humble for Your sake.

O Jesus, I love You. (September 6, 1935)

Polishing the Surface

"By your patience, you shall gain your soul." (*Lk 21:19*)

Beloved, how true this is. I often rebel at the "medicines" You send me, but daily, I understand better that seemingly simple saying, "God uses people, things and events to teach us and test us."[40] How could I learn unless through the daily polishing of my surface by different contacts? All this happens in Your goodness. Teach me to accept it as such, Beloved. Teach me to be always humble in my behavior with others, for they are so much better than I. Teach me to be tolerant and happy, to hide my troubles, and to give others no trouble. O Jesus, make me worthy of the name of friend and follower. I love You. (September 12, 1935)

The Charity of Christ

"The charity of Christ presses us." (*2 Cor 5:14*)

Beloved, how I understand this! The charity of Christ pursues me and encompasses me from all sides. Indeed it does! I stand aghast before its width and depth. Every day it whispers, sings, points out to me something new: He did this for you; He suffered that for you; He lived this way and tired Himself for you. Before me, day after day, passes the life of my Savior, overshadowed and over-laden with love for me. I see it all—from the humility of Nazareth to the agony of Calvary.

And I? This is my eternal question, "And I?" When I look at my life, so much of it is still worldly, uninteresting, wasteful. Beloved, I want to love You. I want to be all Yours, to die to the world for You. Help me because alone I cannot do it. Help me to save my soul and then the souls of others, Beloved!

(September 13, 1935)

The Path to Love

"No man can serve two masters." (*Mt 6:24*)

Beloved, I discovered this to be true a long time ago. I have realized the impossibility of doing it, and am trying hard to give up the world! But the world seems to have so many tentacles. I have been thinking a lot about the way to sever all connection with it.

I know it is a slow, inward process. I must detach myself from all inordinate affections. By this I mean all affections that keep directing my mind toward the world. I must face it fearlessly and unafraid.

You, who know my soul, know what I have to fight. Will You please help me, Beloved, to sever the last strings. I have understood and walked the path of detachment from material things. Wealth does not attract me, nor does power, nor position in the world, nor fame. A burning desire for poverty is in my heart! I love You, and my hourly prayer is to love You more. Now I have to supernaturalize my attachments to all who are a part of my life. Help me, O Jesus, You who give us such a wonderful example.

Give me also the grace of slowly reducing my life to the bare necessities, not conspicuously, but in a hidden, quiet way. Above all, detach me from the spirit of the world—the blame and the praise! Let me receive the first as a natural due, the second as due to Your glory. Let me walk the path of life hidden in Your Sacred Heart, doing all this for love of You and for no other reason.

O Jesus, how full my soul is of determination and desire to serve You and You alone in love. But look at my weakness.

Look at my unworthiness. Take pity on Your child and walk with me, for without You I am as nothing.

(September 15, 1935)

A Lamp to Guide Me

"He who follows me, walks not in darkness." (*Jn 8:12*)

"Your word is a lamp to guide me and a light for my path." (*Ps 119:105*)

Beloved, it seems I will never tire of trying to understand Your words! Each time I read, a new meaning, a more profound shade, a depth unnoticed comes to light. How I love You and every word You spoke and every little thing You did, Beloved Jesus! But it's not enough for me to love. I must imitate, follow in Your footsteps. Even though in my earthliness I can do no better than a deficient imitation, there is Your grace! With You, I can do all things.

O Jesus, help me. Give me Your silence, Your meekness, Your humility. I want to follow in Your footsteps.

(September 20, 1935)

Remember You Shall Die

"O Lord my God, enlighten my eyes that I may never sleep in death." (*Ps 12:4*)

Beloved, how seldom we think of death! Yet, it is all around us. And although, to any Christian, death is a "coming home," nevertheless it is impossible to think of it without awe and fear, for death is also Your judgment on our soul! If I were to die right now, how would I stand before You, O Lord and God? Fear overtakes me at the mere thought of it. On one side, my life shows all the light, graces, gifts and love that Your mercy, goodness, generosity have given and sent me. On the other, are my own free will's reaction to Your gifts!

Jesus, give me tears, for I am a wretched sinner! My sins rise to confront me and to show me up. As I look upon myself, all I can do is repeat the cry of the leper, "Master, make me whole,"[41] or the prayer of the publican, "Have mercy on me a sinner!"[42] Beloved, I cry to You: give me tears. Give me the resolution to mortify myself while there is still time.

O Jesus, have mercy on me; have mercy on me, my God and Lord. Holy Spirit overshadow me that I may sin no more. For it is through Your grace alone that I can keep away from sin.

Beloved, I have wasted so many years. Give me the grace to devote to You my whole life from now on. Long or short, let every moment of my life be Yours. O Beloved, I love You. Give me strength to prove it. O Jesus, my God, my love, my all!

(September 22, 1935)

You Have Been Made Precious

"You are not your own; you are bought with a great price." (*1 Cor 6:20*)

I never realized this as vividly, as profoundly, as I do today! Indeed, I belong to You. For Your Incarnation, Your hidden years, Your ministry, Your Way of the Cross, Golgotha, are all for me, to save me from eternal death, O Beloved!

What more can men and women ask? God not only loves them, but loves them unto death, and urges them to love Him after He has proven His love by death on the cross! Mystery of mysteries—the incomprehension of human indifference! But Master, although I am nothing, in another way I am precious. You have made me so by dying for me!

Take my heart, Beloved, and allow me to love You for the many who do not love You. Allow me to atone for those who do not pray, and to suffer for those who mock and crucify You anew in their hatred. Take my life and my love for atheists, for those lost, wandering souls who never seem to know that light is so close to them! O Jesus, how I want to bring men and women to You—many, many, many! Beloved, give me the gift of absolute love for You, expressed in love and service to my neighbors—without a thought, without hesitation to give all, even my very life for them. You died for them!

(September 27, 1935)

My Most Precious Gift

"Will a person gain anything if he wins the whole world but loses his soul?" (*Mt 16:26*)

Beloved, make me realize that my soul is the most precious part of me, Your most generous gift. Make me realize that it is eternal—that by obeying it, cherishing it, saving it, I can come to You, my beginning, end and all! Make me realize that it is so precious in Your sight that You died for it. It is the seat of all love and beauty. Make me realize that, and when I realize it, live up to it.

Jesus, never let me exchange eternity for the world, even when it calls with a loud voice and the misfortune of sin has touched my soul. Do not allow me to delay a moment; let me run to wash it in Your precious Blood. Lead me on the way of union with You, the only safeguard against the world. Detach me from all created things. Lift me up to Your Sacred Heart!

(October 1, 1935)

A Lover of Christ

"Be concerned, above everything else, with the Kingdom of God." (*Mt 6:33*)

What a great marvel is this that we, vile and unworthy human beings, are allowed—nay urged—to live for You and even to die for You, our Lord and God!

How often I have pondered this truth! Yet I never cease to marvel at it. Beloved, is there anywhere, in heaven or on earth, any creature that has so many privileges! You came down from heaven to save us. You died for us. You are with us in the Blessed Sacrament until the end of time. You are a beggar for our love.

How can we resist all this glory and serve someone else? My soul sings to You a song of thanksgiving. Here I am, all Yours, to serve and love and die for You if You will have me!

(October 4, 1935)

Do All in God

"Without me, you can do nothing." (*Jn 15:5*)

Beloved, how true this is! Only in You can things be accomplished. Help me to go on trusting and abandoning myself to Your providence. I love You! I want to be all Yours and work for Your poor. And since it is Your work, why should I worry? Alone I am nothing. In You, all things are possible to me, for You are God! Prostrate, I adore You and leave my work, myself, and my life in Your hands. Teach me that even overcoming myself is possible in You. Having realized this, let me begin with faith and courage. You know my poverty. But in You I can do all things. So, dear Lord, help me to carry on and bless me! (October 9, 1935)

Let This Be My Glory

"I lift up my hands to You in prayer; like dry ground my soul is thirsty for You." (*Ps 143:6*)

Indeed, Beloved, how true this is! I am as a pilgrim lost in the dry desert of life! Beloved, Beloved have pity on me. For I thirst when I look upon You and see You in all Your glory, and then look at myself and see how as nothing I am. I shudder.

You have called me, this insignificance which I am, to work for You, my Lord and God! All I can say is, "Let this be my glory, Lord, to kneel at Your feet and adore You. Let this be my pinnacle of fame, prostrate to fall before You!"

Oh, how I have loved the beauty of Your house, Lord, and the glory that dwells within it! It is not only in Your church that I find it, but in every human being, for are we not all temples of the Holy Spirit? And is there not Your glory dwelling within us? And so I pray I might always see in my fellow human beings just that! Help me, O Lord, to do right! Give me the living waters of Your grace! (October 11, 1935)

An Enormous Sweetness

"Say to my soul, I am your salvation." (*Ps 35:3*)

Beloved, today at Mass, and yesterday, and many times in

the last week, You have granted me an enormous sweetness. It was as if You, smiling at me, were glad to see me. My whole soul thrilled at the feeling.

O Beloved, why do You notice insignificant me? This will forever remain a mystery to me. I will not try to probe it but will just accept it joyfully. A strange gladness prevails in my soul these days. I feel like singing songs of love, adoration, thanksgiving to You. I have counted my blessings and found them without number. You have called me into Your fold, then into Your service. I have had many sufferings, but somehow, they were like a gift from You and I love them. You have given me a life of service, and with it has come peace and joy that transcends human understanding.

I am happy, oh so happy, my Lord, as I have seldom been in my life. I know that my road is yet full of sorrows, misery, persecution. But I also have tasted of Your beauty, and with Your grace, nothing will separate me from You. O Beloved, why have You given me so much? I am such a great sinner, such a vile person, undeserving of all Your gifts, the least of all Your children. I want to cry when I think what I could have been and what I am!

Jesus I love You. I am Yours. Allow me to sit at Your feet.

(October 13, 1935)

A Mother's Prayer

"Abide in my love." (*Jn 15:9*)

Today, my heart is sick for my child. O Jesus, Your will be done. Yet I pray. I pray for him with my whole being.

O Blessed Mother to whom I dedicated him, Beloved Mother, cover him with the mantle of your protection. Help bring him to the feet of your Son.

He is Yours, O Jesus. I pray, do not allow life to hurt him so early. I love him so. He is my child as You were once the child of Your mother. In Your mother's name, I ask. Have pity on me, another mother.

(October 18, 1935)

Darkness

My heart is heavy within me. Somehow all is at a standstill. My heart is like a heavy stone. My will is stationary. My reason is asleep. My soul is slumbering. I love You, yet my love seems to have lost fire. I still work for You, but my work is pale and anemic.

O Jesus, please give me strength. Give me patience. Give me understanding. My vitality has been sapped. It is so hard for me to bear the trivialities of others and I am irritable, despondent, miserable. O Jesus, do not let me go under, please, Beloved. Darkness and light must follow one another. I have asked to be with You on Calvary. And here, as soon as the shadow of the cross comes over me, I wilt as a child. O Jesus, be my strength.

(October 24, 1935)

Hear Me, Lord

I am still in the throes of darkness. The day passes on leaden feet. All seems to turn against me. O Jesus, please help me to bear it all as well as the dryness of my soul. Even the work is distasteful to me. I must make myself go, do, speak. All is profound darkness. I cannot even see the cross but just cling to it blindly.

(October 26, 1935)

True Charity

"If you love me, keep my commandments." (*Jn 14:15*)

Beloved, I try so hard, but somehow I never seem to succeed. I work so hard at Your works of mercy, but I seem to have no charity. Efficiency, kindness, goodness of heart—yes. But I have nothing like real charity—that elusive tenderness and sensitivity to the feelings of others that mark true charity.

O Beloved, when I read about how gentle and kind You were, I see myself as I am. How far I am from that understanding, that profound insight into others that would give me gentleness of touch in healing spiritual wounds.

For the sake of Your poor and unfortunate children, give it to me, Beloved. Light my soul with the gift of prayer. Give me an understanding and practice of humility. Have mercy on me, Master!   (October 27, 1935)

How Hard It Is to Love

"Love one another." (*Jn 15:12*)

O Beloved, how I try to do so. How I desire it and how really hard it is to love some people. Beloved of my heart, give me the grace to love all people and to serve them for Your sake.
(November 4, 1935)

I Live In Faith

With the world as it is today, how could I live otherwise? Atheism, injustice, and greed surround us, spreading their tentacles all through the world. Is there, in the world today, another safe place to go but to You, faith in You? Alone in this friendless world, filled with misery and evil, we can only say with Your disciples, "Lord, to whom should we go?"[43]

The answer is ever before us. We must go to You, who are the bread of eternal life! O Jesus, keep me close to Your Sacred Heart, for the forces of evil are strong and the fight is hard. I feel them so often, so close to me. Great temptations arise in my soul.

O Beloved, let me live in faith, for if faith is taken away from me, nothing is left—just a void, an emptiness. Give me the grace to bring others to You!   (November 8, 1935)

You Satisfy the Hungry Heart

"Turn O my soul to rest, for the Lord has been bountiful to you." (*Ps 116:7*)

Where can I go if it is not to You? The world is a world of shadows. The company of people is sorrowful. In You alone do I find what my soul hungers for. In You alone do I find happiness. Whenever sin enters my soul, discord results.

O Beloved, how I love You. How I long to serve You and be Yours. Help me to fight temptations which are so strong these days. I feel like a soul in torment, buffeted by the winds of evil.

Be with me. Help me, O Lord my God.

(November 12, 1935)

Lord, Give Me Patience

We have to be patient, not only with ourselves, but with events and people outside of ourselves. This is a virtue I have prayed for much! Patience—with all the little irritating things of the day, with the constant difficulties with people. Jesus, give me this gift of serene, untroubled patience—gentle and kind under provocation. (November 13, 1935)

A Child's Trust

"Do not worry about tomorrow." *Mt 6:34*)

How safe one is in Your arms, my Lord and God, how safe and simple. If only people knew the coziness of absolute trust. As for a child in the arms of its mother, there is no worry. It is warm and snug. The winds of worries, the rains of doubt, the storms of passion just pass by.

O Beloved, tomorrow is not mine and yesterday is past. I have only today. Really, only this very minute is my own. Why should I worry about the next? I have only this hour, this day to account for; I have only this time in which to be saved or damned.

O Beloved, give me Your Spirit. Give me Your grace. Give me the profound understanding that You alone are reality. All else is shadow. (November 14, 1935)

Impatience

Beloved, You know my impatience. You know how quickly I tire of all resolutions; how impatient I am about lack of progress;

how tired I become the moment the work I have started begins to run smoothly; how green distant grass looks to me!

O Jesus, help me to be patient, to plod and not to be always snatching at stars. Teach me to plod daily through small irritations, discouragements, knowing it is for You.

(November 19, 1935)

I Wish I Could Shout

"My spirit has rejoiced in God, my Savior!" (*Lk 1:47*)

O Jesus, when I contemplate Your beauty, Your love, Your goodness—when I realize how wonderful are Your Incarnation, Your hidden years in Nazareth, Your death on the cross—my heart rejoices in me and with Your Blessed Mother. I want to sing! "My heart magnifies the Lord, for He has done great things for His servant!"

O Beloved, as the day starts, how often I wish I could shout from the housetops the joy of being Your servant, of living for You, of working for You! What greater happiness can there be? Indeed, my heart rejoices in God, my Savior!

(November 21, 1935)

A Little Peace

Beloved, a little peace came into my heart today, a sunrise, as it were, upon all my doubts, dryness, and misery. My soul is at rest in You and filled with the glory of Your love!

(November 28, 1935)

Your Will Is Mine

Beloved, today, into Your hands, I put my fate. I will not worry any more, just leave it all at Your feet. Whatsoever is Your will is mine. I will pray for light to know Your will and for strength to do it. The rest is in Your gracious hands.

(November 28?, 1935)

A Manger, A Woman, A Child

Incomprehensible as the thought of the Incarnation is to me, I submit my reason and my intellect to my faith.

All I think of is a manger, a woman, and a child. I go there to shed all the notions of reason and let only my heart speak. I love You, Little Infant. Teach me simplicity and humility—the keys to heaven.

O Jesus, help us who are surrounded by so many temptations of flesh and spirit, against whose weak intellect the waves of atheism are forever running. Help us to remain unafraid, faithful, and staunch because of that manger, because of that Infant—the mystery of Love and Life.   (December 2, 1935)

Pain

Beloved, my heart is like a raw, bleeding wound. It is so long that people have tried to hurt it and hurt it again and again. I thought I could stand it better, but no, again they have dealt it a blow and cut to the core! How painful it is. My soul is all like a ball shriveled up because it is bruised beyond endurance! O Jesus, what have I done to all these people? I have never spoken ill of them, never touched them. I go my little way, hidden in the slums, helping whom I can. O Jesus, I do no harm to those who delight in besmirching my character and spreading false rumors about me!

Beloved, I can hide myself only in Your heart. They succeeded in crucifying You. In Gethsemane, and throughout the centuries, they made You sweat blood and tears! If they did that to You, why should I complain about the crushing loneliness of the crucifixion of my inner self, about ridicule of all that I hold holy, about subtle and open persecutions, about trenchant and biting gossip, about indifference.

O Jesus, have mercy on me. Give me strength to go on when my only human thought is to run. Love means the cross. Give me strength to be crucified on the other side!

(December 5, 1935)

You Have Stooped Low and Touched Me

Beloved, indeed You have, for there is not one in this wide earth who is more humble, less deserving than I am. You have stooped low and touched me with Your hand and allowed me the privilege of working for Your poor.

O Jesus, prostrate I adore You and love You. I repeat again and again, help me to be worthy of Your call.

(December 6, 1935)

Joy At Mass

At Mass, a flood of joy! I will never forget this Mass—the closeness of God, a feeling of profound union, a vivid and terrifying realization of my unworthiness, a sense of joy and reverence for being chosen to do His work, a realization of the privilege. I received a thousand glimpses into my only reality. I thought I was in heaven: all my sorrows, all my burdens lifted, just my soul and Him remaining—a lifetime in an hour!

There was a sense of being lost in an Infinity past understanding; a fear and a joy indescribable at His nearness; a magnificat singing in my soul, wordless yet loud; a love for His Blessed Mother filling me completely; and an overwhelming desire to be a worthy child.

"My soul magnifies the Lord for He has done great things to His handmaiden."[44]

(December 8, 1935)

The God of Good Works

"The God of good works must never be deserted for the good works of God."[45]

Here is a perfect truth. I have to pull myself up and remember it. For in the rush of the day, with the happiness that comes naturally from doing Your work, the supernatural is so easily lost from sight. And that, I know, is death, for what would it benefit me to gain the world and lose my own soul?

Keep me, Beloved, within the circle of Your arms. Give me the gift of prayer. Help me to rise above myself, above the din of praise, above vicissitudes, to be always inwardly united with

You. Make me realize You are the beginning and end, and I only a channel. For alone I could not save even a fraction of a soul!

(December 18, 1935)

The Goal We Strive for

"Spiritual life is sometimes spoken of as the seeking after perfection. If this is understood to mean that persons aiming at spirituality are to set before themselves their own perfection as an object after which they strive, it is apt to lead to serious mistakes. Spiritual life may be more clearly, simply, and correctly described as the 'cultivation of intimacy with God.'"[46]

How often we lose all recollection of the good we planned to do when we undertook our spiritual battles! The goal was love and union with You. In it was the reason for all our efforts, for the spiritual life of a man or woman is You. Without You, there is the arid desert of natural virtues without grace.

What does it matter if we pile up Masses, rosaries, novenas. What does it matter if we fast and flagellate ourselves if we lack the self-abnegation necessary to give You full scope to work Your way in us! To study You; to do all things for love of You; to act against oneself for the same motive; to show love in deed to our brothers and sisters, always keeping our spiritual face toward You, always drinking of the waters of eternal life from You, being simple as children: in these is sanctity.

(January 2, 1936)

Hunger for Christ

Beloved, deep inside me I feel arising a new hunger for You. I want to come closer to You, to shed people, as I advance in life. I look around: the world with its shoddiness, its tinsel, is just a cheap side show at 4 AM, bedraggled and dirty in the rainy morning.

Solitude of heart attracts me more and more—friendship with You, my Lord and Master, with all it entails. On my part, I crave, like a tired child who has wandered far, to crawl back into my Father's arms. So few humans understand. Even those close to me prove empty of help and sympathy. They are in no way interested. Some are all self–worry and self–pity regarding themselves alone. Some are understanding but cruel in their immature judgments. It is hard to carry on. So, Jesus, take me close to You, close to Your Heart. (January 11, 1936)

To Change My Life Fully

My soul is happy tonight. At last, I have made a good full confession of all matters that troubled me. Now I am over it and clean before You, without any blemishes. Jesus, I wanted to take this precaution, for I really want to change my life fully, leave the world and serve only You.

Beloved, let this be Your secret and mine. Let this change be known only to me, hidden from the eyes of my associates and friends. Let me work on myself with Your help and grow in love of You! I know now, with a knowledge no one can take from me, that You are the real reality, and all the rest are shadows. In You alone is peace and happiness. I was created to serve, love and adore You. Take me and never let me go. This alone I ask.

Only now do I realize, still dimly, what spiritual life really means. I am afraid of my weakness, but my strength will be Yours. So I pray and ask You to sustain, encourage and help me. For I love You above all else and want You for life. I realize that I have sinned grievously and that I want and must do penance. So I will start at once. I will try with Your help here and now.

Help me Jesus, please. Once more I must face the vices, faults and imperfections I am to fight: impatience, irritability, sarcasm, unkindness in speech, pride, arrogance, vanity, self–satisfaction, smugness, boasting. These are the virtues I must cultivate: humility, silence, solitude, recollection, gentleness of speech and manner, good manners in general, tidiness, severity to myself, no criticism of others in public, understanding and gentleness to others.

You see how almost insurmountable is my task. But the supernatural life is You. And above all things of this world, my soul desires You—to love You, to serve You, to live or die for You. This is my ambition, and on my knees I pray: help me to make it my life's sole work. Help me to keep on.

(January 16, 1936)

I Have Chosen You

Beloved, to come to You I must leave everything and practically everyone! I must always be master of my emotions. I must act either against my natural desire or I must supernaturalize it. I have made my decision, Lord: I have chosen You. To follow You, I must walk a hard, narrow, and steep road. How hard, how narrow, how steep I barely realized until today. But now I know. With Your help, I want to get there.

I love You above all things. I want to be where You are. But I am so rough, so uncouth. I know now that in all things I must show example. I must be kind to others and severe with myself, not defend myself, not become irritated. Teach me to follow You in small and big things.

(January 18, 1936)

I Thought I Was Doing Something

Beloved, slowly I begin to realize things I should have understood so long ago. Before I can start on a life of the spirit, I must shun sin—mortal and venial—and faults and defects. I used to think at times that I was doing something for You! Now I can only see what You are doing for me! I liked to listen to my voice, to the well-chosen, well-rounded words I was so good at speaking. Now I have learned that words obscure some things, and in silence and recollection we find more than in all words combined.

Mortification was known to me but I did not see the inside of it. I begin to perceive it now—the mortification of reason, judgment, will. My soul magnifies the Lord for His great mercies to me. I want to be Yours.

Keep me, O Jesus, and never let me go.

(January 20, 1936)

Active Work and Inner Danger

Beloved, as I realize how little advanced I am in the way of spiritual life, I tremble lest I should fall before I have even learned to walk. What do I know of real mortification, penances, prayer, of the deep and profound spiritual life of Your great apostles?

But I love You, Jesus, and I want above all not to do anything that will separate me from You. I want to work only for Your glory and in answer to Your cry "I am thirsty."[47] Above all, I do not want to work for my glorification or glory.

I feel weak and small, like a baby learning to walk. I want to hold on to Your hand for fear I will fall. I want to be gentle and kind. I feel strange inside. The only secure things seem to be simple things—my little rule and a desire for perfect obedience to it, prayer, simple meditation, and work with You close in my heart and mind.

O Jesus, I love You so! Keep me within the circle of Your altar.   (January 24, 1936)

The Life of Prayer

"The life of prayer, even if it does not show itself exteriorly, is in itself and of itself a source of activity with which no other can be compared."[48]

Beloved, as I try to understand Your way and learn of You, I find many things more clearly etched out. You are the beginning and the end, the reason for and the source of all spiritual life. Prayer is really just talking with You, and the greatest part belongs to You. Our part is to empty ourselves to be filled with You.   (January 25, 1936)

The Road that Leads to You

"Misfortunes of life, storms raised by passions, nothing can make her swerve from the lines of conduct she has laid down for herself—to seek in all things God's pleasure. Besides, if she stumbles for a moment, she pulls herself together at once and goes marching forward more steadily than ever."[49]

O Lord, am I equal to a life like that? I don't know. I only know that I love You, that this is the path I must travel to reach You. It seems so steep to me, so lonely, so inaccessible! But what does it matter, it is the path You want me to take. I am already on it with my two feet!

I know I will fall, scratch, bruise, hurt myself and cry because of fright and loneliness. But I also know You will be there to help me. So here I am, Beloved, an utterly unworthy servant, yet one who loves You. Bless me on the road that leads to You, and do not allow me to get lost, even for a moment.

Jesus, my Lord and my God! I have no one to go to, Darling. I am so tired, so miserable inside. Let me come to You and hide myself in Your Sacred Heart. You will understand, for You have said, "Even if your mother should desert you, I will not desert you."[50]   (January 28, 1936)

Deliver Me from Self-pity

Jesus, You know I have no friends. I have followers and acquaintances, but no friends, no one interested in my doings, no one interested in me as I am.

Today, I have had an overdose of it. You know what I mean, Beloved. Perhaps it is Your way, to detach me from people. While I still have time, what would You want me to really do?

Jesus, help me please. Above all things, deliver me from self-pity, from whining. I come to You because it hurts and because I love You. And, if it is Your will that this dark loneliness be my trial and my fate, Your will be done, Beloved.

Be my strength. I love You.   (February 1, 1936)

I Know the Way Is Prayer

Beloved, I want to come to You; I know the way is prayer. Teach me how to pray to You with my lips, with my intelligence, with my mind, and with my will.

O Jesus, to pray to You is to speak to You. To speak to You is to learn to know You. To know You is to love You. To love

You is to follow You and to follow You is to surrender one's self. Jesus, at all cost, lead me along Your way!

(February 4, 1936)

His Fullness

"Of His fullness we have all received." (*Jn 1:16*)[51]

Indeed, in all the sacraments You enrich us, but in the Blessed Eucharist, You simply overfill us with graces. Woe to me if I do not correspond to them. For if I want to be Your apostle, first I should learn interior life and then come to the world filled with Your Spirit, to be a channel of Your Spirit! O Jesus, help me to be full of Your fullness, which You give with such generosity.

(February 5, 1936)

The Soul of an Apostle

"Light ought to flood the soul and inflame it...so that reflecting this light and this heat in turn, it may enlighten and inflame other souls."[52]

Beloved, Your apostle is all light and love and fire for Your sake and on Your behalf. Help me to reach that stage where my very face reflects You! O Jesus, I love You. I want to help others to love You. Make me travel that road of love which is the one of rigid self-control and discipline. Let me lose my soul for You and find it in others! Jesus, I love You!

(February 6, 1936)

I Want to Do It Right

Jesus, I want so much to do what is right because I love You! It is the deep irresistible force that comes from the Blessed Sacrament that sends me out daily happy and content. O Jesus, I love doing Your work, but I want to do it right. Help me. I know it depends on interior life!

(February 7, 1936)

Be a Cistern

"If you are wise, be a cistern..." (St. Bernard)[53]

Now and then, as I see glimpses of the interior life, I begin to realize that the path to You is rocky, desolate, lonely in appearance. I also know that it is made easy and beautiful at times by Your felt presence, sweetened by its grace. I know it calls for absolute surrender, self-abnegation, self-effacement, abandonment, complete trust and faith, humility, mortification and penance.

O Jesus, it is a hard path for flesh and blood—impossible without Your help. O Jesus, You know I love You! You alone know my sinfulness, my imperfections, faults. Help me, above all, in courage. I want to walk Your way. Here I am. Make me a saint even if it breaks me in the making. I want to be filled with You as a cistern is filled with water—clear and cool in the desert of life. I want to fertilize Your fields, forever overflowing with Your Spirit, the Spirit which alone can bring men and women to You! (February 11, 1936)

Fighting Temptation

The great heat of temptation again comes near. Jesus help me. Help me to fight it. Beloved, just now when my mind is under the influence of a strong temptation, I have only one safety belt, and that is the rigid adherence to my rule of life. Yet my mind seemingly refuses to be dislodged from its malady.

O Jesus, how powerful are our senses and how hard to subjugate! I know it only too well. Give me strength to fight.

(February 15, 1936)

See How Small I Am

"To see in everything, habitually and simply, the will of God."[54]

Beloved, how simply Your saints looked at life! Here I am, crushed to the ground by the misery of sad news. I seem to ask so little, just to work in Your vineyard—hidden, unknown and peaceful. None of these three things is given to me, O Beloved. Of course I make mistakes, but who does not.

Jesus, see how small, how weak I am. I cannot work alone. How tired I get. How little I am prepared to see Your hand in all things. And out of my nothingness and weakness, You are trying to do Your work.

O Lord of Hosts, I am the greatest sinner on two feet. For I see the grace You gave and which I have squandered, lost, trampled underfoot! Look and behold one whom You have redeemed with Your Precious Blood, one whom You have covered with Your graces as with precious stones, one whom You have called to do Your work!

O Jesus, Master, have pity on Your unworthy servant. One thing only can I say, "I am ready, my Lord, ready if You want me as I am." (February 28, 1936)

My Love Shoots Up

Beloved, again that beatific feeling of being in Your presence has pervaded my soul. I feel so peacefully at rest, so gloriously happy. Indeed, I feel like the apostles—"Lord, it is good for us to be here."[55]

At Your feet I rest in a peace that transcends words and surpasses understanding.

In that peace, thoughts come to me that do not otherwise appear. I see the world torn away from You. I see the curse of its misery from having denied and rejected Your existence, and its yearning for You as never before!

Then I contemplate my own sins. The enormity of them makes me shudder. In the light of Your presence, their hideousness is revealed in all its clarity. How little I have done for You; how mixed my intentions are! O Beloved, above all, have pity on me, have pity on me. A lifetime will not be enough to erase my sins.

Like a flame, my love for You shoots up straight and clear, overshadowing all the rest. It is exquisite agony to love You, Lord, because my poor love falls so short of what love of You means. Like a prisoner stretching his chains to the breaking point toward freedom, my soul stretches its arms toward You, vainly trying to break from the shackles of flesh.

O Jesus, Son of God, I adore You with all my soul, my mind, my body. I pledge myself to Your service in whatever shape You want. I have read the writing on the wall. I know that loyalty to You might mean martyrdom in the near future. I am only a weak woman. But with Your Holy Spirit at my side, I hope to be strong even unto death.

Jesus, Son of God, I love You with all the love a poor, broken, sinful human heart is capable of. I love Your poor because You said You are in them. I pledge to dedicate my life to them for Your sake. I believe in You and in the whole teaching of Your holy spouse, the Church. I pledge myself to honor You with her liturgical voice, to obey her unto death, to pray for her, to help her. She will need every little crumb of help so soon. Jesus, Son of God, I am Yours now and forever. If, in my weakness, I fall, lift me up. If I fall, encourage me, for I am alone. I love, I believe, I adore Your divine will in all things. Amen. (March 14, 1936)

Like a Shaft of Light

How clearly, while I was walking yesterday, I saw all that is wrong. It is I. If I want peace, charity, kindness, love of God to reign, I have one way open to it: to be all these things myself!

O Jesus, how long it takes for a person to see! Yet the solution has been under my eyes all the time! Where from, my terrible blindness? O eyes that see not and ears that hear not! I wonder if I will ever get anywhere.

Suddenly this perspective opened before me. Like a shaft of light piercing the darkness, I saw why all was as it was—because I was not what I am to be. All my sins rose from the past like dark shadows and pointed their fingers at me. Then came a desolation—such as I had never known—into my heart and soul, and with it, an overwhelming sorrow.

I could not resist; I changed the course of my walk. For I felt impelled by a force I could not resist to run to Your house, to kneel at Your feet, to pour out my soul in tears and in sorrow for having offended You so much.

O Jesus, words cannot describe the feeling, the light that shone on my sins. You saw how it was. My soul wept at Your feet. I wept and resolved to put all things aside as it is my vocation to do—to be in the world, but not of the world—to strive to lift myself up.

I will not go in for outward things, Beloved. I will go in for inward things! What does it avail me if I fast and am unkind, if I pray and am sarcastic. From now on, I will strive to change my rebellious heart, subdue my pride, master my intellect for Your sake and service.

In general, I will try hard to be an example in all things. O Jesus, help me. This is the hardest road yet which I have undertaken to travel. Help me! Help me! O Beloved, help me.

I will also strive to pray more, to cultivate the sense of Your presence, to develop a hunger for You. O Jesus, how deep are Your ways! (March 15, 1936)

Being Holy Means Loving You Much

O Jesus, my Lord and God! To realize Your Passion is to realize the emptiness of the world. The world has nothing to offer. You have all, O Beloved. I love You. Teach me to love You more! I am a great sinner, an unworthy servant, but I love, love, love, love You!!!

Increase my love, increase my fervor, increase my holiness. I want to be holy, for being holy means loving You so much! I feel You in my heart. I walk in Your shadow. You are my life.

(April 8, 1936)

How Beautiful You Are

"Active life is employed in works of devotedness. It treads the path of sacrifice, following Jesus, who is worker and pastor, missionary, wonder-worker, healer and curer of all—tender and weariless—helper of all the needy ones here below."[56]

Beloved, the more I live, the more vivid is my realization of You. It is as if, daily, You come closer to me in Your humanity. Daily, I see Your beauty more and more. Daily, the path You followed becomes clearer to me and my desire to follow You more irresistible.

How beautiful You are! I desire to follow You, even unto Calvary. Make me see and understand, and give me strength to do as I see and understand. O Beloved, I am Yours. I dedicate my life to You in following You among the poor!

(April 10, 1936)

Let Me Be Faithful in Little Things

Jesus, again the burden of dryness and difficulties is on me, but I want to carry on through it. When You are not with me, all things are so dark. Just now I have no excuse since You really are so very close, so terribly close to me in the tabernacle.

Let me be faithful in little things. Let me be faithful to my rule, and accept meekly all rebuffs and difficulties. O Jesus, I love You. Let me show this love in fidelity to little things.

(April 20, 1936)

The Cycles of Life

Slowly, my life is coming into its own, resuming its happy rhythm of work and prayer. I worry about so many things that the only thing I should worry about—the salvation of my soul—recedes into the background.

Today, anew, like an ever-repeating miracle, I see the renewal of my love for You and I realize more than ever my privilege in serving You.

O Jesus, I love You and ask only one favor—to love You every minute more and more! (May 23, 1936)

Am I Being Presumptuous?

Beloved, I want to be a saint. Is this presumptuous? I do not think so. You want us to be perfect. Besides, a saint is one who loves You. I want to be a great lover of my God, to do all things only from love of You! Make my intentions perfect!

(May 25, 1936)

I Must Get Up and Follow

In my meditation, things slowly become clear to me—Your life, Your teaching, You. Slowly You reveal Yourself to my soul. Your beauty unfolds itself so that my soul cannot remain still. I must get up and follow You, Beloved! Love for You begins to burn my soul! It consumes it with a desire for You.

O Beloved, I love You; teach me to love You more and more! I want to be a saint. I want to follow You through the dark, loathsome ways, through steep hard paths, because You alone are God. You alone possess the words of eternal life because You loved me unto death. (May 27, 1936)

Save Me from Blindness

Jesus, keep me from this terrible condition—to be spiritually blind—not to see because I have overshadowed my eyes in sin and negligence. Teach me to see, to hear, to be sensitive to the slightest sin. I love You so. Please help me.

Beloved of my soul, today I want to hide myself in Your heart and rest a while, just rest, like a tired child on its mother's breast. I am weary of so much noise, tired of so many people. I want to be alone with You for a while in silence and solitude. Help me to get there. Help me to do Your will. (May 29, 1936)

The Lord Is Not in Noise

How well I feel that when Your presence seems especially close. During the day, instinctively, I want to walk quietly, lower my voice. It jars me to hear noise then. It is as if it were not respectful.

Jesus, how quiet, tranquil, and peaceful is Your spirit. Teach me that I might truly walk in inward and outward peace. It is a great desire of mine of fulfill the motto: "Walking in love and peace, we do all things to bring all men and women back to Christ."

Jesus, how good of You to allow me to serve You.

(May 30, 1936)

Peace and Happiness

Slowly, the inner life is unfolding before me. I have worked hard this week to be punctual at all my exercises of piety. I have ruthlessly overcome the desire for pressing activity. I have fought the strange distaste for vocal prayers that has been with me for so long. I have garnered, through Your mercy and Your kindness, much peace and happiness!

Today, a great peace and contentment stole over me. It was a peaceful scene. The world was so far away with its noise, its rushing, its movement so opposed to Yours, Beloved. Today, I understood better than at other times the glory of Your service. A great song of thanksgiving rose from my heart to You, my Lord and Master, for having allowed me to come near You.

Beloved, Master, how sweet is Your name. Jesus, Jesus, Jesus! It seems as if there is infinite happiness in repeating it again and again! (June 1, 1936)

We Are Offshoots of God

O Jesus, how important interior life is. How could it not be? What is it but Your life in us and ours in You. A person of interior life is one who realizes You are the vine and she a branch.[57] Yet, do we ever think about what it means to be the branches of such a Vine? The same sap flows through the branches as through the Vine. We are offshoots of God! Unbelievable, incredible, yet profoundly true because of God's infinite mercy and goodness. (June 3, 1936)

Give Me Wisdom, Lord

Indeed, it is at Your feet that we learn wisdom. O Jesus, teach me. I long for the peace and calm that You alone can give.

Help me, Jesus. Help me to learn from You, to go about my business through the day in Your presence.

Beloved, You are the light and the life of my soul. Teach me to follow You.   (July 7, 1936)

Help Me to Take Life in Little Bits

O Beloved, in Your infinite mercy, how good You are. Help me to go through life daily, no matter what the disappointments may be, always hand in hand with You. Let me remember to take my day in little bits, remembering that the duty of the moment is Your duty. Let me face sorrow, disappointments and betrayal with gratitude, remembering that You had to face them all.

O Jesus, help me. In You is my strength.   (July 8, 1936)

I Come to Rest at Your Feet

Divine Jesus, have mercy on me. I come to rest at Your feet, Beloved, to take stock of the years just passed, to face the year to come in the light of Your love and service. I have chosen to give my whole life to You, Beloved. I have chosen to belong to You. Jesus, have mercy on my poor service; help me to do better in the future.

My loneliness is great. I have come again to ask help to carry on. I have come to pray for all who have asked me to pray. I have come to rest, to strengthen myself, to ask You for sanctity, because sanctity is love of You.

Jesus, I went to confession for all the sins of my past life. I am free of them—all washed white! Pure heart, Mary, take my white soul into your hands and never let it go.

Around the corner, I must meet new temptations. Let it be God's grace to keep me from them. Mary, Mother of God, help me to be pure; give me a shining devotion to you.

(August 1, 1936)

Blessed Shall You Be

"Blessed shall you be when men shall hate you, when they shall revile you and persecute you, when they shall separate you and shall reproach you and cast your name out as evil for the sake of the Son of Man and speak all that is evil against you unduly, for my sake. Be glad in that day and rejoice, for your reward is very great in heaven." (*Mt 5:12*)

Let me fully understand the truth of these words. In them lies the secret of meekness and understanding. I should walk unafraid through life, as long as I walk for You, Beloved!

My heart is Yours. I want it so, Jesus. Today, through all the pain and discomforts of the body, I have seen Your face. I want You to have all of me!

Jesus, Mary, Joseph, take me with You to Nazareth. As to all the difficulties, these I will leave to You, Jesus, and in all things, do only Your Will. (August 2, 1936)

All That I Have Is Yours

You have asked something of me that is hard to give: take it. It is Yours. I do not want to keep it back! I want all that I have to be Yours. You understand all, Jesus. I want to keep back nothing. For I want to live and die in You.

Beloved of my heart, I have sinned so much; there is so little time left to atone. Do not let me sin again. Help me to be good.

O Jesus, I love You above all things and I wish to be Yours. I put my heart into the hands of Your mother today. Ask her never to allow me to take my heart back to myself no matter how often I ask. (August 2, 1936)

Take Up Your Cross

O Jesus, I desire to follow in Your footsteps. I desire with all my heart and soul to take up my cross, the one You have prepared for me, and to follow You.

O Jesus, my love, let me begin by doing all things for the love of You, all my little and big actions, all things! Be at my side all day. (August 4, 1936)

I Have Put My Trust in You

O Jesus, my God and my all, You are my only trust. I put all my hopes and trust in You alone. I am alone in the world, O Jesus. Help me, for without Your help I can do nothing.

Jesus, my heart is full of love for You. I offer all my actions to You in love—every little thing I do. (August 5, 1936)

You Are Joy

"The sacrament of love ought to be that of joy."

O Beloved, indeed, how could it be otherwise, even in all the difficulties? For if I possess You in the Eucharist, I enjoy Your real presence and its sweetness! You alone are food and drink and the only joy in this world! You are joy! Your service is one of joy!

O Jesus, if only people knew what delight is in Your service, they would all become Your slaves, Your servants, Your friends, Your brothers!

O Jesus, indeed my soul is filled with the joy of Your service. I love You. Today, I offer You all my actions for love—only love! Teach me to see, Beloved. Teach me to understand that love alone can be my motive in Your service. Beloved of my heart, Infinite Joy, let me be Your humble servant. (August 6, 1936)

I Feel So Alone

The effect of five days without meditation due to pressure of work is apparent. My spiritual life is at a low ebb. I am, as it were, all misty inside. Gone is my clarity of vision, my surety of purpose! All things are indifferent to me. O Jesus, help me. Please help me, Beloved. I feel so alone.

Jesus, please, I love You. Help me! (August 16, 1936)

Dark Clouds Surround Me

My heart is heavy, O Lord. Dark are the clouds around me. There is nothing to do but to let You handle it all. I leave myself entirely in Your hands. The nails penetrate deep and my heart is bleeding. O Jesus, I love You. I love You. Help me, a sinner.

(September 4, 1936)

All Is Pain

Lord, I cannot meditate. All is pain—heart, soul, and body. Help me to retain sanity. That is all I ask. I love You in spite of all and will bear all for Your sake and for the church. Jesus, I am in a tight spot. I have no friends, just You. To You I turn, offering You all for Your sake. (September 10, 1936)

The Message of the Gospel

It seems to me at times that we complicate Your lovely, simple, free teachings so much. Each time I read the Gospel, I am overwhelmed by its simplicity and beauty. I am overwhelmed also by the difference between what You preach and what is. It is so sad. O Jesus, give the world light!

(September 24, 1936)

You Mold Me with Suffering

Beloved, indeed You are forming me. Blessed be Your holy hands, for You are molding me to suffering. Forgive, dear Lord, my being impatient at times. Forgive my weak complaining and my desire to turn away. It is the human, the weak quality in me that rebels. But what there is in me of the spirit rejoices and is at peace. I love You so. I love You with all my heart and soul.

(September 26, 1936)

Real Success

What is real success? It means following in Your footsteps. It means suffering for love's sake. It means that great and wonderful peace that You alone can give. It means being lifted up to You, by You, crucified on the other side of Your holy cross and seeing the whole world at one's feet—realizing its need, loving it unto death in You, for You and through You!

O Jesus, let me be even a little success that way, even though I will be a complete failure to the world.

(October 1, 1936)

Human Darkness

My heart is heavy because of our human darkness. I love You so. I see the darkness within myself and others. We try, and we strive, and we work and worry, yet all the time we live in strife and misery within ourselves. Our souls are full of noise! We should live in peace and holy tranquility, but do not allow enough time for reflection. Make their souls quiet, dear Lord. Please make mine quiet. I love You.   (October 2, 1936)

I Await Your Pleasure

O Jesus, faced with wrack and ruin of all my work, with—humanly speaking—crushing humiliations and difficulties, I have only You to come to.

I thank You, on my knees, for the great peace You have given me these days! I thank You for the sense of detachment You have put into my heart, for the absolute submission of my will to Yours. I can say, in all truthfulness, that I am ready for an absolute failure in the worldly sense.

You have before You my intentions, my little efforts, my love for You—such a poor, weak, human love, so full of streaks of weakness, so tragically inadequate—yet love all the same. I do my poor best, with failings, mistakes, sins and pitiful efforts. You alone know it all, Beloved. You know what awaits me. You know my crosses. All these things I lay at Your feet, and await Your good pleasure. Ahead of time, I submit to its decree.

What is a good name, or honor, or glory, before Your cross and Your absolute nakedness? Where the Master is, there shall the servant be.

Bless me, dear Lord. Forgive my sins. Help me to be true to You. The rest is immaterial.   (October 9, 1936)

Be My Rock

Beloved, I am but a weak, unworthy woman, with no one but You to really turn to! How far away I am from all those strong souls who can be like rocks!

O Jesus, the only thing I can do is throw myself at Your feet and pray that You be my rock. All I have to offer You is my love, a broken, pitiful love, a love stained with the dust of earthy roads, a love smeared with the darkness of sin. When I lift it to You, how pitiful it looks in Your heavenly light. That poor, broken thing I have to give You, and with it, myself—also not much, just as pitiful and broken as my love!

I have more things to put at Your holy feet—my little, puny efforts to be and to do good. Jesus of Nazareth, Master of souls, look at them. Those efforts of mine are like broken pieces of glass, baubles of poverty.

All this I dare to bring to You, my God—to You, King of Kings, surrounded with gifts of spotless souls, heroic love, mighty efforts!

I know it is pitiful! I know they look so small and insignificant. Forgive me, dear Lord, and help me to do better. Do not send me away, for without You there is only death and eternal darkness. (October 10, 1936)

Forgive Them, O Lord

"Who abides in me and I in him shall bear much fruit." (*Jn 15:5*)

O Jesus, much sorrow is in my heart today. You alone know the reasons and intentions with which I have worked on Your behalf these last two and a half years. You alone also know the hearts of my enemies. You have seen how they have condemned me without investigations, without questioning, and so forth. You see the injustice of it.

But You also know, as I do, that I am a great sinner and deserve it all, and more. Daily I have wondered why You tolerate me on the holy ground of Your vineyard. So You know well that I realize I deserve it all.

One favor I ask of You, Beloved, that my heart be absolutely free from bitterness—that it might not harbor even a shadow of vindictiveness against my persecutors. Forgive them, O Lord, for I forgive them from the depths of my heart. Lover of souls, have mercy on me, a sinner. (October 16, 1936)

How Helpless We Are

How helpless, selfish, and weak we are! You alone can kindle fire in our hearts. O Jesus, You alone can lift us up and give us the courage to be crucified in the process because of love.

I have searched the earth for love and found the love of human beings very weak, shallow, and insipid. I have lifted my eyes from the earth to heaven and found You, Beloved, and my love has found a nest for herself. Only in loving You has human love also become great and beautiful.

O Jesus, Beloved, I love You. And because I am nothing without You, be my strength, my courage, my all.

Beloved, give me the strength to go on; give me the courage to assume my burden anew. Walk by my side! Teach me to be an example to my associates, and especially to love all my enemies. Jesus, in my love for You, let me be true to You.

(October 18, 1936)

The Gift of Prayer

Beloved, I come to You and ask for the gift of prayer. If anyone needs it today, I do. I need to pray because my world is toppling all around me. All is darkness. I stand clinging to the cross. Everyone else is gone.

O Jesus, have pity on Your child. The darkness within me is greater than the darkness without. I am as a lost ship. It is hard to pray, harder still to go to Mass. O Jesus, have mercy on me, a sinner. In You is my last hope. (October 27, 1936)

To Suffer Like the Saints

O Jesus, prayer is hard, but to us ordinary human beings, suffering is harder still. Beloved, I am suffering now as I have never suffered before for Your sake.

Help me! I am really not a saint nor cut out to be one. All I do is love You. You know the temptations that assail me. You see the battle I am waging now, when all about me is crumbling, all is darkness spiritually, all is pain physically. I do not know where to turn.

O Jesus, take pity on Your unworthy, distracted child. I love You! (November 4, 1936)

To Keep Faith

Beloved Lord, one thing I ask of You: allow me to keep my faith! Let me keep it before the terrible injustices of today, the indifference of Catholics, the worldliness of the Catholic clergy. I feel the temptations mount and mount and mount. It is all so bewildering, Jesus. I want to cry! (November 7, 1936)

A Shadow of Peace

A shadow of peace came to my soul. Dimly, far, far away, I see a little pinpoint of light. But as yet, all around me is impenetrable darkness. I struggle in vain to pierce the hole and can't. So I give up and rely on the will of God, drifting I do not know where or when. His will must be enough for me from day to day. To glance at my life just now bewilders me. Inward pain is there all day from it all. Jesus, have mercy on me, a sinner.

(December 26, 1936)

What Is Your Will?

A quietness has come into my heart as if in answer to my prayer. It is a time of peace in which my mind is beginning slowly to grope through the maze of the tragedy, darkness, revilement and persecution that have come to me in the last six months—months of blessings—if only I could but see it all.

I know I have to make over my life; from now on, it seems my lot is to be a hidden one. Will I be able to start my life once more so I can rest peacefully in one place and do good?

Jesus, what is Your will for me? You have taken away so much; You have given away so much. I know all this is a blessing, but I cannot see it yet.

Please guide my steps in this New Year, and do not allow me to stray from Your path, Beloved. Help me to do the right things. (December 27, 1936)

Weariness

More and more my heart and my soul retire into themselves. A great feeling of physical weariness has come upon me; I am so very tired. In the very inactivity of my tiredness, there comes a feeling of quietness. Noise, continuous action, and all contact with the world are far behind me. It is as if I have gone into an inner retreat where I have time to look back on the past years, where I have a moment to look into my own soul.

The light that confronts me is not very encouraging. If You were to look for a greater sinner, You would not find one.

Jesus, to You alone do I dare to lift my eyes, for You alone are all understanding and all merciful. To You alone can I lift my voice: "Lord, have mercy on me, a sinner."

Do You want me to cleanse myself now, in this period of silence, oblivion and retreat? If You do, lead me, Christ. For You alone possess the light that will illuminate the dark corners of my heart and make me see and hear, and seeing and hearing, act. In You, then, do I put all my trust! (January 3, 1937)

I Want to Scream

Dear Jesus, must my soul always be steeped in suffering? Again, yesterday and today, it came over me like a wave. So many things seem so difficult—poverty, insecurity, the terrible injustice done to me. Jesus, my love, can I go on?

O, I know the problems of suffering. I know the mystery of success through failure. But tell me, Beloved, why am I so terribly lonely, so tragically lonely? Why must I always be in pain and live the way I do? No friends—really, no one loves me. People ask so much and give so little!

Beloved of my soul, why? Why is life such a lonely thing? It seems to me, at times, an unbearable burden. I come to You; I pray. But my own sinfulness stands in the way. It is as if my window were opaque and would not let the sun through.

I am so alone at times when You are far, Beloved. Today is a day like that. I feel tortured with fire and pains of such strange, inexplicable tortures that I want to scream. Instead, I am silent. O Jesus, have mercy on me. For today I am in such darkness, such spiritual sorrow, such pain. I want to cry. O Beloved, have pity on me a sinner. I cry to You out of the desert of my life.   (January 6, 1937)

Jesus, I Am Sorry

O Jesus, how weak, how sinful I am. Listening to the sermon today, I realized more than ever how hard it is to follow Your will and how necessary. I write about uncompromising Christianity and I myself compromise all the time. I speak of Your crucifixion in the hearts of men today, and I drive the sharp nails of sin into Your holy palms harder than anyone.

Day in and day out, I am a hypocrite. I love You and betray You in one breath. The more I see the world, the more I see myself. The more I go about "my Father's business,"[58] the more I realize what a poor servant I am and how poorly I attend to it.

Vain, vain-glorious, with a great opinion of myself, with a desire for adulation; weak, unstable, uncharitable in many ways; lazy, good for so little, prone to all human passions. O Beloved, how can You bear with me? Blaming others for hurting me, yet inflicting hurts on others. Jesus, Jesus, have mercy on me a sinner.

There is only one way of doing Catholic Action and that is to begin with one's self. The first step is uncompromising Christianity. O my soul, let it start with me.

Jesus, I am sorry; for the hundred millionth time I am sorry. I will try again. Give me the grace to do so. Without You, I am nothing. Only You can give this weak, poor heart of mine the strength to begin once more. (January 10, 1937)

Prayer for Priests

Today I looked at Your priests. I came to You in Your church and prayed for them that they might become busy about our and their Father's business.

I prayed for myself, too, that every minute of my day might be Yours, Beloved, and that the light of the Holy Spirit might bless my humble new apostolate. I prayed that every word of mine might be spent at Your service as the candles before Your altar give light.

O Jesus, the world has forgotten You. What can I do but pray and pray again, Beloved. (January 13, 1937)

On the Edge of Despair

Dear Lord, I will never make a good servant. Look at me! Early in the morning I'm tired, dispirited, miserable, filled with worldly ideas of ease and luxury. I desire never to get up early, to have breakfast in bed, and to live in sloth and ease. I am so tired, dear Lord, I want to sleep all the time. I do not want to see people, go out, or do anything but sleep. Every effort, every person annoys me, and it is with difficulty that I restrain myself.

I am only at peace when I am alone with my thoughts and dreams. I still feel bruised, and the fresh wounds smart. I am so tired of mere living. I want to be alone in a little house in the slums and live there by myself.

O Jesus, what a worthless servant You have in me. Instead of forging ahead, working for Your kingdom, I do so little, daily, hourly, minute by minute—with indifference, as a ghost, and with a tiredness that begins at dawn and never lets me be until dark.

Jesus, have mercy on me a sinner. (January 20, 1937)

The Hunger Is in Me

How tenacious Your love is. If I try to change, to draw away from You, if the tinsel of the world seems under some strange light as gold to me, how gently You follow me. How finely, with all gentleness, You draw me back. Indeed the human soul was made for God! I will never be satisfied with less. The hunger is in me. It fills me at times like a mighty flame. It lifts me up and consumes me. Help me.   (February 2, 1937)

The Dark Night

What is it I want from life? Why this loneliness, this terrible pain and bewilderment? As so many times before, my whole life seems to be breaking up. All my work is going on, but it is quite obvious I am not wanted, and it hurts. All I can think of is how terribly tired I am. Master of life, help me to understand this terrible pain. I am willing to bear it for Your sake, for the sake of Your people, for my brothers and sisters.

All I ask, Beloved, is that You be by my side and give me the strength to move one spiritual foot in front of the other, for I am so terribly alone just now. Truly, all is terribly dark.

Still, I have not answered my question. What do I want of life? If I let an immediate answer come I would say, "Peace, a few years of happiness." For Lord, as You know, I have never known such years since I left my father's house. The years after my childhood have been all shadows. Always. I ask for neither gold nor silver, nor fame nor renown nor power. I don't! I ask for peace and a little sunshine. Is that too much? Perhaps it is. Therefore, I will simply say, "Your will be done in me, not mine."   (April 1, 1937)

Jesus, How Can You Stand Me!

The night was dark. I lay awake. Does anyone understand the horror of dark nights, when all is quiet as if it were dead? I faced the past and shuddered; the future and shrank. Seventeen long years of pain and suffering, seventeen years of hell, and nobody knows! Indeed, I am a failure in all things—in married life, in motherhood, in my work for humanity.

Lord, as I think of all these failures, I wonder if by any chance it would be possible to find anyone who has made a bigger mess of life than I. I am sure not! Jesus, who are the Master of all things, how do You stand such as I?

Oh, I am not complaining about my fate. How could I? For all that has come to me is well-deserved because I am such a sinner. My sins are always with me and before me, as are the graces I have lost. I often think of these graces. Are they lying there, crying, because I haven't made use of them? Or have they been picked up by chance? Who will know the end of this mystery? Death alone will solve it.   (April 25, 1937)

Jesus, I Want to Be Yours

Again and again I fail You, Beloved. And yet You pursue me and bring me back. Why?

How passing is the moment of sin; how eternal is Your peace. Why must we sin? Why do we sin when Your beauty is so complete? What is there even in the best the world has to offer to attract a soul who has caught a glimpse of You? I see the incomprehensible perversity of the world, the incomprehensible folly of men and women.

Yet, here I am, having tasted Your friendship, caught a glimpse of Your beauty, understood and possessed Your peace. Weak and sinful, I fall again and again to the lure of this world. What am I to do? From the very depths I cry to You, my Lord. Have mercy on me, have mercy! In the midst of my falls, my efforts, my sins, my desires, my heart is filled with love for You. Can it be? I am attracted to You so powerfully. I want to serve You and love You and be Yours.

Beloved, I must follow You by getting up from my fall, bruised and battered as I am, full of the dirt of my fall. I must come to You again and, penitent, be made white and clean.

I love You Jesus. Yes, I, a vile sinner, love You. Slowly I divest myself of all things to come to You. Direct my path. Help me to find myself; help me to do what I think I must do to be Your own! Jesus, I want to be Yours! (April 30, 1937)

A Burning Grace
What is this inner hunger I feel so much except the grace of God? How lasting, how deep-seated it is, and how it burns like a fire. At times it eats me up, literally.

I have to speak of it, put it into action, write of it. Only I do not speak of it as my hunger. I am too shy for that. I just call everyone I meet to come to Christ.

Oh, I am more subtle than the evangelicals. I do not say outright, "Brother, be saved." But perhaps I mean the same thing. What I want to say is something like this: "Stop, wait a minute. Look around and see Christ. There He goes in that tired, listless worker who has tramped all day in search of work. Here He stands at the corner. Look there; look at that beggar who looks so derelict that no one even wants to stop and listen to his low, whining voice. Can't you see the weary face of the Nazarene glance through those lustrous eyes? That ragged boy who runs heedlessly into the path of a roaring truck is Christ also. Don't you remember Christ was a boy once? His feet are ill-shod and cold. His little face is pinched and hungry-looking. He is one of the millions of children of the slums. Come with me to the slums. We have them everywhere. And there you will see Christ multiplied a million times. Oh, friend, stop, look, and think. And then go and pray and love and help. For it is your love alone that can release Christ in the hearts of thousands who have forgotten Him because of poverty and injustice."

I want to say this for it burns like a fire in my heart. But, often, I do not do it well. But always I do it for Him whom my heart loves. (December 27, 1937)

I Have Come a Little Closer to Christ

Another year closed. As I look back on the year, I see much pain, much suffering, and great joy. It seems to me, that in spite of my sinfulness, I have come a little closer to Christ; I see His face a little more clearly. And, seeing His face, I see myself a little better.

Here, as I pause and look deep into my heart, I must admit to a feeling of fear and near trembling. The graces given to me were many; so many were God's gifts to me. And how little use I made of them!

How loudly I have spoken throughout this past year of the faults and failings of others, especially the clergy. And how little I have done to correct my own!

Lord, have mercy! I have, in the depths of my heart, suffered in my pride, and have mistaken these sufferings for some real woe. How little do I know of the elusive virtue of humility. And yet, one look within me ought to annihilate me completely!

All I have to say for myself, as I look at the past year, is that I have tried—alas very badly—to love and serve God, and through Him, my brothers and sisters. I could have and should have done better. Alone, dear Jesus, I cannot. But with Your help, I will try again. (December 30, 1937)

The Silence to Hear Your Voice

What is this—for me—strange desire for quietness and prayer and meditation? I want to be very still, not even praying with my lips—just to sit at Your feet, my God, and listen to the great silence in which You seem to whisper to my heart.

There are so many things I want to hear from You in that silence; yet I must go back into the rush and turmoil of life. But, as I think of it, I see a way out. And that is to keep deep in my soul—within the rush and turmoil—that great silence and peace in which alone we poor mortals can clearly hear Your quiet voice. We are so weak that alone we can do nothing, not even keep silent in our souls in order to hear Your voice.

For the New Year that comes—so full of possibilities of serving You—I ask three gifts, in memory of the Three Wise Kings. I ask for Your protection of my son, for the grace of that silence that will allow me to hear Your voice, and for the courage to do as Your voice will guide me. Amen.

(December 30, 1937)

O Jesus, to Make You Loved!

How beautiful the Mass is! At times one can almost feel the presence of Our Lord. And after Communion there is such love, awe, such a sense of the Infinite in one's heart, that it seems impossible that so many people do not know Him, or, what is worse, know about Him but do not believe in Him. The pity of it! A great desire comes into my heart to go forth at all cost and tell them about Him, make them love Him.

Then, dark and forbidding, the cost comes clear to me—misunderstandings, persecution by one's own, stripping of all things human beings value, including honor. Each step is wrought with suffering, sacrifice and pain. I know it from personal experience. And yet, after Communion, when I go back deep down within myself and adore God there, nothing seems to matter—only Jesus and the stupendous love He bears us.

Jesus, I love You. Sinful, poor, of no account, I love You. I have tried to run away from Your love. You remember that night when I decided to make the break and become an average, ordinary Catholic? The other kind paid to high a price for their originality, I thought. You shook Your head and said: "No, Catherine. You know you belong to me." That was all. A flash. A second. And all things fell into their proper proportion.

You remember that evening, Jesus of Nazareth? It was the turning point of my life. My heart removed itself further and further from the world. And You helped me through people and circumstances and brought me into Your work. And I have been there ever since. Your Spirit lit the fire that is burning even today in my heart.

- 136 -

Dear Lord, help me never, never to quench those flames that burn and sear my soul. Let me always be about my Father's business, for this is the acceptable time. (January 18, 1938)

Forgive Them, Jesus, As I Forgive Them

"They who sow in tears, shall reap in joy." (*Ps 126:5*)

"Then shall they deliver you up to be afflicted and shall put you to death; and you shall be hated by all nations for my name's sake." (*Lk 21:12,16-17*)

So, dear Lord, this is the fate of Your followers. By this shall it be known that we belong to You! We always have to reap in tears here on earth in order to reap in joy in heaven. And they will put us to death, and we shall be hated by all nations. And then many will be scandalized and betray one another and shall hate one another.

Is this not what is happening now, O Beloved? Are not all those who love and serve You really hated and persecuted by those who should help them? Terrible is the fate You predict for Your followers!

This morning at Mass I was afraid. But I know there is no other way! So, Lord of Hosts, I stand before You, a beggar for all things—courage, perseverance and, above all, love of You. Love knows no limits to sacrifice, and, in love, we receive courage and perseverance. Beloved, give me a great, overwhelming love of You, and the rest will be added to my poor, weak, and sinful heart.

This morning, I prayed again for my enemies and offered Mass for them. There are so many of them I cannot remember them all. But I especially prayed for those who have steadily persecuted me. Some I have never met, but they speak of me so badly. For them and for all the others, I ask Your blessings. Forgive them, Jesus, as I forgive them. For who am I to hold any grudge? If they judge me mistakenly in one way, they are right in a general way: I am a sinner. So nothing they can say will be too much. I love them dearly. You, who know my heart, know that. Amen. (January 19, 1938)

Can Your Heart Throb with Pleasure, Lord?

Can it be really true, Beloved, that You crave our love? Yesterday, reading Reverend Leen's book, *In the Likeness of Christ*, I came across this passage. It made such a profound impression on me. "Nothing can oppose an insurmountable barrier to His love, except...our free will. He looks anxiously for the first stirring of that will, its first feeble attempts to respond to grace, and as He notices them, His heart throbs with pleasure. He craves our love..."[59]

It's almost incredible, Beloved, that Your divine heart can throb with pleasure when we sinful creatures turn our hearts to You—our hearts which have been fashioned by You, whose every beat is in Your hands, You who came on earth and died for our salvation!

Yet, patiently You wait on our pleasure, because with life, You have given us that sublime gift—free will. All things of love are a free gift!

Jesus, how profound, how incomprehensible this mystery is. What hope it gives us sinners, to me, in particular, who seem to understand all this, and yet, so often (oh, You and I alone know how often) stray into other paths which, if not forbidden, at least take me away from You. Always, You send grace after me and bring me back as that lost sheep in Your parable. And not content to call me back, You put me on Your shoulders and bring me back.[60] What should I do in the face of this infinite goodness? I should fall down, adore You, and never get up. I should give my whole life to You and never so much as look at other things!

What, Beloved, do You want me to do? Whisper a little tiny word to me, O Beloved, so I can do Your holy will. I am ready to give up all things for You. You know that, even though at times I falter and fall. I do not want that free will of mine to ever stray from You! You are my all, my life, my love, my goal. You alone are truth and life and my door to eternal life, which will be bliss only if I live it near You. Jesus of Nazareth, have mercy.   (January 20, 1938)

- 138 -

The Fire in My Soul Will Not Let Me Be

O Lord, Lord, why have You given me Your gifts? Why have You given me this clarity of vision, this imagination that makes me see You in all the poor, the lame, the halt, the blind? Why is it that my heart cannot rest? Why do I want to be where I am not? Why am I drawn to leave all things and follow You, even when my flesh, blood, mind, heart shrink from the thought, and only my soul sings and sings eternally the song of poverty and renunciation? Why do I have to feel like that now, after having given You years of my life, and finally having been squashed?

What do I do, knowing as I do so many delights of Your company, having walked and talked with You so often? The graces You have showered on me! And why me who, of all Your many servants, am the most unworthy?

When I think of what You have done for me, and then look at what I have done for You, I want to cover my face with my hands for sheer shame. I want to run away, sink through the earth, disappear forever from Your glance. But I know there is no place where I can hide from You.

So will You, Beloved, forgive Your wayward child once more and hide me from myself in the only safe place—Your Heart? And never let me go, always allowing me to correspond with Your grace.

O Lord of Hosts, I stand before You with a heart full of tears and a soul filled with repentance for all the moments I have been away from You. Sins of my past life stand before me in all their horrible nakedness. And I have only Your mercy to fall back upon. But then it is an infinite mercy, so I throw myself into its sea and swim to the shore of Your love.

O Christ of the Poor, O Christ of the Worker, still that raging fire in my soul. I am sorely afraid. I tremble in every limb. Jesus, be my guide. Stop my tears. I weep because I am afraid, but the fire in my soul will not let me be.

(January 24, 1938)

To Do All Things with Your Blessing

O Jesus, I have learned that only when I do Your will in all things and start everything with Your blessing, do I find in my actions happiness and peace—Your peace.

Help me, Lord, always in all things—to do them with You, to pray over them, to ask Your blessing, and to keep before my eyes the pure intention of loving You and doing all things for that love and Your greater glory. (March 9, 1938)

What a Privilege!

Lord, how I wish I would love You as the saints did, and really work for You. The good souls think that I am "heroic" because of where I live and the work I do. But You and I know that far from being heroism, it answers a sweet compelling invitation from You, and is such an alluring, delicious, heavenly adventure for me!

Every morning I wake up with the thought that the day is all Yours. It is like a continual birthday party in which anything could happen! Souls could be brought to You, groups formed, momentous meetings held; it is such a privilege, such a joy!

O Lord, if they think this "heroic," they don't know You. This is a continual privilege, honor, adventure, full of glamor. Thank You every day for the joy—the strange intoxicating joy—of serving You in Your poor, of being allowed, sinner that I am, to walk with You and talk with You in them!

(March 18, 1938)

The Light of the World

"I am the Light of the World." (*Jn 8:12*)

Jesus said this two thousand years ago. How evident it is today! All these poor people who do not believe in God; they seem to me so many blind folks who do not want to see. Chaos surrounds us; the abyss confronts us! Yet all we do is as if to apply a mustard plaster to a cancer, knowing full well that only a major operation can save us!

It seems so simple, so absolutely clear: our salvation is within us. We do not have to go to any extreme, for our problems are ethical and moral, not political or economic. If only we would restore Christ within our hearts, and abide by His laws of love, all would be settled!

O Jesus, give us light, Your light, to lighten our dark hearts.

(March 29, 1938)

How Lovely Is your Service!

Beloved, how lovely is Your service! Every day is like a fresh new day; every day is useful—spent for others. How can I ever thank You for the privileges and gifts You have showered on me. Today at Mass, the wonder of it all came back with a new beauty, and dazzled me again! True, long, dreary, and dark are the days in between. (Or are they centuries?) But when a day like today comes, there is joy that blots out and overshadows all the rest.

Beloved, I love You. Teach me to love You ever more.

(April 6, 1938)

How Simple Things Are!

Beloved, how simple things are, and how complicated we make them! Your laws are sufficient to us, to give us real lasting happiness and peace. Yet the one thing we do not try is to practise them! Why? It is because they spell always self-sacrifice and self-forgetfulness. Can't people and nations see that in these very words are hidden all the things they seek? Is their blindness willful? Or is it just ignorance?

O Beloved, daily I thank You for the grace of sight—inner sight—that You have given me. Forgive me my sinfulness and weakness that lead me to shirk some of the directions of that sight. Daily I pray for strength to fulfill all your desires and commands. Bless this day and all my days; allow them to be spent in Your service.

(May 3, 1938)

Real Peace Is in You

Beloved, there is real peace in the world; it is in You. Who but You could give this immense inner peace that comes on soft feet to quieten into holy tranquility a heart surrounded by the noise of continual action. It is as if my soul becomes a cool, quiet temple, standing in the shade of eternal trees, alone—an oasis in a broiling sun.

O Beloved, how peaceful You are! How quiet! How tranquil! How strong! The voices of the world die into silence at the threshold of a soul filled with You!

Give me Your peace! I love You; teach me Your holy quiet strength! Beloved, I love You! (June 18, 1938)

Afterword

Catherine Doherty was a woman of many facets. She was a woman of deep pain, intense joy, passionate love, and exceptional energy. She was a woman of fun and laughter, and a piercing intellect. She was a superb organizer who took delight in the lowliest of tasks. She rubbed shoulders with the famous, yet had tremendous sensitivity to the poorest of the poor. Her mother told her, "You were born under the shadow of the Cross." Looking now at the fruits of her apostolic life, we know something more: Catherine died in the light of the Resurrection.

Several times in her life Catherine was plunged into the despair of deep rejection: when she fled her country, when she left her husband, at the closing of Friendship House in Toronto, and when she left Friendship House in the United States. Again and again she was cast into crushing loneliness and massive experiences of failure.

In the 1930's, she suffered the rejection of priests. In 1951, and again in 1981, she was personally encouraged in her apostolate by Popes.

By the time she died, there gathered at her bedside dozens of members of the new apostolate she had founded, Madonna House, and she was mother to a host of spiritual children all around the world.

Time and again, her "failures" proved to be anything but sad, dismal endings to her apostolate and spiritual quest. As the Lord's plan unfolded, each "failure" opened to her a much broader range of vision and a much larger set of opportunities for loving than before. Not only that, she was able to communicate that vision and pass on her inspiration to a multitude of others.

To Catherine, the experience of pain, persecution, death, or desolation wasn't ever the most important thing. She was in love with a crucified Lord. She longed to be like him, to be crucified with him. What mattered to her in the midst of her apparent failure or her pain was that she continue to find meaning in his suffering, that she continue to listen to his beloved voice. In him she always found new hope, new spark, new light, new joy.

In her prayer we see her returning constantly to spending time alone with the Lord. She turned to the sacraments and to scripture as the wellsprings of her spiritual life. She strove to live always in the presence of her Beloved, and the events of his life were the key in which she found meaning and purpose in her life.

Catherine's spirituality and approach to the Gospel were never merely theoretical; they dealt always with the very practical demands of love and extended to the most humble details of everyday life. As people gathered around her, she founded Madonna House, whose members seek to live out her vision of Christian life. Over the years literally thousands of people have been inspired, set on fire, born anew as they have visited Madonna House. Under Catherine's influence, young and old, lay and cleric, men and women of many cultures, Catholic and not Catholic, have dedicated or rededicated themselves to love of God and are pouring out their lives in his service.

Catherine left a large body of writings, in which she strove to articulate God's voice as he called her and formed her apostolate and her life. She wrote to the members of her apostolate as a group and individually. She spoke to them during spiritual readings. She spoke frequently in public. She conducted a voluminous correspondence with missionaries and individuals throughout the world. The Madonna House newspaper, *Restoration*, contains many articles by Catherine, and she wrote a number of books—on the situation of the Church, on Russian spirituality, on Madonna House life, and on prayer. Much of this is available now in published form in several languages, through Madonna House Publications.

In all these ways, Catherine's message of the Gospel goes forth to places and persons far beyond the physical presence of Madonna House and its members. Because she embraced the cross with such daily passion and determination, she showed to anyone who saw her, read her writings, or received her letters the central message of the Gospel. She showed them the heart of Christ, the word of God in human flesh who loves us, saves us, and transforms us. It is the endeavor of Madonna House to continue to do this.

Of course, the full story of Catherine's influence, the complete roll of persons whom her words and life will inspire, are not yet known. In fact, on this earth, they will never be known...

Notes

1. *Jn 19:28.*
2. *The Virtue of Trust*, Paul de Jaegher, p. 14.
3. See *Mt 25:21.*
4. *Mt 26:41.*
5. Quoted in *The Virtue of Trust*, p. 27.
6. *The Virtue of Trust*, p. 28.
7. *Jn 19:28.*
8. See *Mt 25:14-28.*
9. *Mt 25:40.*
10. *Jn 14:15.*
11. *The Soul of the Apostolate*, J. B. Chautard, pp 14–15.
12. *The Soul*, p. 20.
13. *The Soul*, p. 22.
14. *The Soul*, p. 53.
15. *Jn 19:28.*
16. Introit, Holy Thursday.
17. *Mt 16:24.*
18. *Jn 19:28.*
19. *Lk 23:42.*
20. *Jn 13:34.*
21. *The Soul*, p. 16.
22. *The Soul*, p. 41.
23. *The Soul*, p. 12.
24. *Abandonment*, J. P. de Caussade, p. 53.
25. *Mt 16:16.*
26. *Abandonment*, p. 62.
27. *Abandonment*, p. 70.
28. *Abandonment,* p. 96.
29. *Abandonment*, p. 98.
30. *Abandonment*, p. 101.
31. *Abandonment*, p. 110.
32. *Abandonment*, p. 117.
33. *Abandonment*, p. 130.

34. *Abandonment*, p. 134.
35. *Abandonment*, p. 140.
36. *Abandonment*, pp 142-3.
37. *Abandonment*, p. 146.
38. *Abandonment*, p. 156.
39. *Mt 7:7.*
40. See *The Soul*, p. 17.
41. *Mt 8:2.*
42. *Lk 18:13.*
43. *Jn 6:68.*
44. *Lk 1:46-48.*
45. *The Soul*, p. 10.
46. *Progress Through Mental Prayer*, Edward Leen, pp 8-9.
47. *Jn 19:28.*
48. *The Soul* p. 28.
49. *The Soul*, p. 30.
50. *Is 49:15.*
51. Quoted in *The Soul*, p. 53.
52. *The Soul*, p. 53.
53. Quoted in *The Soul*, p. 54.
54. *The Soul*, p. 61.
55. *Mt 17:4.*
56. *The Soul*, p. 74.
57. See *Jn 15:5.*
58. See *Lk 2:49.*
59. *In the Likeness of Christ*, Edward Leen, pp 213-214.
60. *Lk 15:4-6.*

Sources Cited

Chautard, J. B., *The Soul of the Apostolate*, auth. trans. J. A. Moran, 3rd American edition, Abbey of Gethsemane, Inc., Trappist, Kentucky, 1941.

de Caussade, J. P., *Abandonment*, or *Absolute Surrender to Divine Providence*, rev. and corr. by H. Ramière, trans. Ella McMahon, Benziger Brothers, New York, 1887.

de Jaegher, Paul, *The Virtue of Trust*, P. J. Kenedy & Sons, New York, 1932.

Leen, Edward, *In the Likeness of Christ*, Sheed & Ward, New York, 1936.
Progress Through Mental Prayer, Sheed & Ward, New York, 1935.

Plus, Raoul, *God Within Us*, P. J. Kenedy & Sons, New York, 1924.

Quotes used with permission.

Note regarding quotes from former publications of P. J. Kenedy & Sons: ©1996 Official Catholic Directory published by P. J. Kenedy & Sons in association with R. R. Bowker, a Reed Reference Publishing Company, New Providence, NJ.

Other Writings by
Catherine de Hueck Doherty

Apostolic Farming
Dearly Beloved — 3 volumes
Dear Father
Dear Seminarian
Donkey Bells
Doubts, Loneliness, Rejection
Fragments of My Life
The Gospel of a Poor Woman
The Gospel Without Compromise
Grace in Every Season
Journey Inward
Lubov
Molchanie
My Heart and I
My Russian Yesterdays
Not Without Parables
Our Lady's Unknown Mysteries
The People of the Towel and the Water
Poustinia
Re-entry into Faith
Sobornost
Soul of My Soul
Stations of the Cross
Strannik
Urodivoi
Welcome, Pilgrim

Available from:
Madonna House Publications
Combermere, Ontario, Canada
K0J 1L0